ASIAN DEVELOPMENT

The Asia Society is a nonprofit, nonpartisan public education organization dedicated to increasing American understanding of Asia and its growing importance to the United States and to world relations. Founded in 1956, the Society covers all of Asia—22 countries from Japan to Iran and from Soviet Central Asia to the South Pacific islands. Through its programs in contemporary affairs, the fine and performing arts, and elementary and secondary education, the Society reaches audiences across the United States and works closely with colleagues in Asia.

The *Asian Agenda* program of The Asia Society seeks to . . .

- Alert Americans to the key Asian issues of the 1980s
- Illuminate the policy choices facing decision-makers in the public and private sectors
- Strengthen the dialogue between Americans and Asians on the issues and their policy implications.

Asian Agenda issues are identified in consultation with a group of advisors and are addressed through studies and publications, national and international conferences, public programs around the U.S., and media activities. Major funding for the Asian Agenda program is currently provided by the Ford Foundation, the Rockefeller Foundation, the Andrew W. Mellon Foundation, the Henry Luce Foundation, the Rockefeller Brothers Fund, and the United States-Japan Foundation.

ASIAN DEVELOPMENT

The Role of Development Assistance

by John P. Lewis

THE ASIA SOCIETY

UNIVERSITY PRESS OF AMERICA

LANHAM • NEW YORK • LONDON

University Press of America,® Inc.

4720 Boston Way
Lanham, MD 20706

3 Henrietta Street
London WC2E 8LU England

Printed in the United States of America

British Cataloging in Publication Information Available

Co-published by arrangement with
The Asia Society,
725 Park Avenue, New York, New York 10021

Library of Congress Cataloging-in-Publication Data

Lewis, John Prior.
Asian development.

(Asian agenda report ; 7)
Bibliography: p.
1. Economic assistance—Asia—History—20th
century. 2. Asia—Economic policy. I. Title.
II. Series.
HC412.L45 1987 338.91'095 87-21599
ISBN 0-8191-6590-5 (pbk.)

All University Press of America books are produced on acid-free paper which exceeds the minimum standards set by the National Historical Publication and Records Commission.

Contents

Foreword

Born of the economic turbulence of the 1970s and early 1980s—which resulted from two rounds of oil price hikes, mounting inflation and a prolonged recession—major changes are occurring in the financing of growth and development in Asia. Most notable are two contrasting trends: a substantial increase in international bank lending to developing countries, especially during the late 1970s and early 1980s, and a decline in the rate of growth of overall levels of foreign aid. Despite a slowdown in the rate of growth of bank lending since 1982, most Asian developing countries now have greater access to external finance than they had a decade ago. But they also face development and debt management challenges aggravated, in part, by the growing scarcity of international aid resources which particularly affects the poor countries of the region. In response to these changes, the countries are having to adjust their development strategies and goals.

The United States has a major stake in how well the Asian developing countries manage the changes in financing trends. As of mid–1983, U.S. bank claims on these countries amounted to some U.S.$31.8 billion, which was close to 27 percent of total U.S. bank claims on all LDCs. Total new U.S. direct investment in Asia in 1983 alone exceeded U.S.$13 billion. And, in the last few years, U.S. trade across the Pacific has come to surpass transatlantic trade. It is currently estimated that every U.S. $1 billion of U.S. exports supports 25,000 jobs. In 1985, Asian developing countries alone accounted for some U.S.$27 billion of total U.S. exports. Moreover, the United States has major security interests in Asia and those interests are intricately tied to political stability in the region and, in turn, to continuing economic progress.

This report is part of a public education project sponsored by The Asia Society to explore the changes taking place in development financing in Asia, their effects on Asian development prospects and U.S. interests and their implications for American public and private policies. The project focuses on four major issues: the changing patterns of development finance in Asia; the experience of debt management in Asia and prospects for future commercial borrowing; the past, present and future roles of external assistance in Asian development; and the development strategies and financing prospects of India and China in particular. The geographic scope of the project is the developing countries of South and Southeast Asia, excluding the so-called newly-industrializing countries (Singapore,

Hong Kong, Taiwan and South Korea) and the socialist economies of Indochina.

The project on "Financing Asian Growth and Development" has sought to provide balanced analysis and discusssion of the issues through commissioned reports and papers, an international conference and regional public programs around the United States. This examination of the role of development assistance in Asian development by John P. Lewis of Princeton University is one of three major reports being published jointly by The Asia Society and the University Press of America. A companion report on the broad patterns and trends of Asian development performance and financing by Gerald M. Meier of Stanford University was published in September 1986. A report on China and India jointly authored by Robert F. Dernberger of the University of Michigan and the East-West Center and Richard S. Eckaus of the Massachusetts Institute of Technology will be published in the fall of 1987. A fourth shorter paper on the role of Japan in financing Asian development by Yasuhiko Torii of Keio University will be published as an Economic Briefing this fall as well. These publications and several other shorter papers were originally prepared as background for an international conference held in New York on September 26–28, 1986. The conference brought together 70 Asian and American economists, policymakers, bankers, journalists and educators to discuss Asian economic and financial issues. Immediately following the conference six of the Asian participants traveled to six American cities where they participated in programs for local world affairs groups, business associations, universities and the media.

This report by John P. Lewis is the seventh in a new series of reports produced by The Asia Society's national public education program on contemporary Asian affairs, "American's Asian Agenda." The Asian Agenda program seeks to alert Americans to critical issues in Asian affairs and U.S.-Asia relations, to illuminate the choices which public and private policymakers face and to strengthen transpacific dialogue on the issues. Through studies, national and international conferences, regional public programs in the United States, and corporate and media activities, the program involves American and Asian specialists and opinion leaders in a far-reaching education process. Asian Agenda publications emphasize short, timely reports aimed at a wide readership. Other Asian Agenda reports address a variety of topics including the Philippines and U.S.-Philippine relations; the United States and the ANZUS alliance; Japan, the United States and a changing Northeast Asia; and the role of Christianity in modern Korea.

The Asia Society is deeply indebted to many individuals and

organizations for the assistance and support that made possible the project on "Financing Asian Growth and Development." First, we are very grateful to the report authors—Professors Meier, Lewis, Dernberger and Eckaus—whose enormous knowledge, experience and insight, as reflected in their superb papers, have provided the substance of the project. Several members of the Society's Asian Agenda Advisory Group, especially John P. Lewis, Dwight Perkins and T.N Srinivasan offered valuable advice and support from the outset of the project. The greatest credit for the overall framework of the project must go, however, to Catherine Gwin, now at the Rockefeller Foundation, who as a consultant to the Society in 1984 thoughtfully defined the most important issues to be examined.

Major financial support for the project came from the United States Agency for International Development (USAID), the Asian Development Bank and the World Bank. The Asia Society wishes to thank particularly Charles Greenleaf of USAID, President Masao Fujioka of the ADB and Shahid Javed Burki of the World Bank, all of whom took a special interest in the project. Staff support for the project was also made possible by generous grants to the Society's Asian Agenda program from the Ford, Rockefeller and Luce foundations and the Rockefeller Brothers Fund.

Several members of the staff of the Society's Contemporary Affairs department played key roles in the development and execution of the project. David G. Timberman was central to the design and early organization of the project. Timothy J.C. O'Shea, David Claussenius and Linda Kojabashian carried it through to completion. Eileen D. Chang carried complete responsibility for the editing and publication of the project reports. Superb administrative assistance came from Andrea Sokerka, Rose Wright, Lorraine Kaye and Emily Collins.

Marshall M. Bouton
Director, Contemporary Affairs
June, 1987

Executive Summary

Official development assistance (ODA) is nonmilitary aid given to developing countries by donor governments, either bilaterally or via multilateral institutions, with the overt purpose of promoting development. Such aid has been going to Asian countries since soon after World War II. Questions surrounding the nature, functions and effectiveness, first of aid in general, then of development assistance in Asia, are complex. But they can be answered with some confidence.

Aid takes various forms—project aid; nonproject aid, including program and sector assistance; commodity aid, including food aid; and technical assistance. Development aid can convey information and influence as well as resources, but all of it in some measure is a financial transfer. By convention, an official transfer qualifies as ODA only if its terms contain a grant element of at least 25 percent. Although all development aid purportedly is intended to be of developmental benefit to the recipient, nation states are not charitable institutions. They give bilateral aid, typically out of one kind or another of self interest—strategic, political, commercial, sometimes humanitarian and sometimes reflecting the donor's stake in keeping an aspect of the global system in working order. In contrast with the complexity of their bilateral motivations, donors jointly mandate such multilaterals as the World Bank to engage in single-minded development promotion.

Both bilateral and multilateral aid will be with us for some time. The former on average has the larger grant element, but both are quite "soft"; multilateral is much more likely to be available for global bidding, untied to purchases in a particular country. Bilateral aid sometimes is more innovative, but the allocation of multilateral assistance among recipients is far less politically motivated; thus it is more responsive to the greater need of the poorer countries. By the beginning of the 1980s the multilateral fraction of total ODA had risen to the neighborhood of 30 percent. Since the ratio has flattened. This is of particular concern to Asian recipients, since, whereas during 1981–1983, 31 percent of the ODA received by all low-income countries came from multilaterals, 45 percent of the Asian low-income countries' ODA was multilateral.

Although critics and defenders of development assistance always are arguing over the policy's effectiveness (aid, an inherently awkward undertaking, seems to be held to more exacting standards than most domestic programs) the debate intensifies when, as now, the budgetary restraints on the activity have tightened. Two recent assessments, both careful, albeit by evaluators closer to the pro- than the anti-aid lobby, deserve attention. In late 1985 the twenty-fifth anniversary report of the "club" of traditional governmental donors, OECD's Development Assistance Committee (DAC), digested the findings of its members' (and of the multilaterals') official evaluation units. About a third of aid's capital projects, according to these assessors, are highly successful, a third are satisfactory, and a third are disappointing (10 percent of the total were rated a total loss). Moreover, emphasized the DAC report, a learning experience has been underway. Both donors and recipients know much more than they did fifteen or twenty years ago about how to give and receive aid constructively. Also in 1985 a Task Force on Concessional Flows representing eighteen governments (nine from the North, nine from the South; eleven donors, seven recipients) reported along similar lines to the Development Committee, the committee of finance ministers jointly attached to the World Bank and the IMF that had set the task force in motion three years earlier.

Of particular interest in the Asian context: the Task Force on Concessional Flows, after struggling with how, in a scarce-ODA world, to cope with the preemptive claims of Africa, unanimously concluded that the two Asian giants, China and India, which have been recording relatively positive development experiences lately, are still too poor to be denied significant access to ODA. "Concessional resource allocations to these large poor countries . . . should not constitute . . . a penalty for performance."

* * * * *

Asia, along with Latin America, is where development aid got started. At the end of the 1940s and during the 1950s it was mostly an American initiative. Indeed, there are some U.S.-centered ironies in the story. For example, early documentation shows that Washington intended that major capital transfers to developing countries should be effected through multilateral, not bilateral channels. But three early cases established the opposite tradition. In Taiwan, once the Republic of China was run out of the mainland in 1949, the United States felt the need to supply major resources without waiting for a multilateral concerting of effort. In Korea, where the formula of 66–percent-U.S., 34–percent-non-U.S. support for the United Nations Korean Reconstruction Agency (UNKRA) had been established, the postwar needs for aid were so large that there was no way to raise 34 percent of the requirements from non-U.S. sources. And in India a large ad hoc wheat loan was made bilaterally in 1951.

The U.S. India program, formally started in January 1952 as the direct result of President Truman's Point Four concept, was something of an exception as it evolved during the 1950s. As in the case of Sri Lanka, the motivation of the India program was mainly development driven. This was possible (despite the fact that John Foster Dulles concurrently was inveighing against Nehru's nonalignment) because the U.S. government, like others, is not monolithic. In particular, American aid-to-India technocrats had great success in sustaining the momentum of their program once it was launched.

The motivation for most U.S. country programs in the rest of Asia was thoroughly political, however—in Taiwan, Korea, the Philippines, Indonesia, Thailand and Pakistan, not to speak of Indochina and Iran. The last two can be left out of account for our purposes: the politics failed, but not because the aid failed. But the further irony is that in most or all of the other politically motivated cases, the U.S.-led aid efforts were *developmentally* effective. As the text puts it, "The story of aid in Asia should prove to any development purist that development assistance does not have to be either bountiful or high-minded to be useful."

The donor agency bureaucrats and technocrats who have been engaged in Asian development cooperation during the past forty years—the U.S. bilateral people, who have been the most numerous in the field, the other bilaterals, the World Bank, the Asian Development Bank and UNDP—have been averagely purposeful and competent. Similarly, most of the regimes they have assisted have been not only strongly but sensibly committed to development—as can be said, for example, of Taiwan, Korea after Syngman Rhee, Indonesia after 1965, Thailand, Bangladesh, Pakistan, but with sharp regime-to-regime changes, and India.

The Asian record provides a variety of perspectives on the interplay between two functions that aid programs can play, one as a deliverer of resources, the other as an influencer of recipient government policies. Both functions have been active in Asian programs from the beginning. At first they were not tightly joined; experimentation with "policy conditioned" capital assistance (especially in various nonproject forms) began to appear in the 1960s, for example, in aid to India, Pakistan and Korea; and now 'policy-based lending' is as fashionable in Asia as in other developing regions. Many instances of positive and negative interactions between donor transfers, donor advices and recipient policy decisions can be identified in the various country cases. At least two general conclusions emerge: (1) episodic impacts on policy have not been inconsequential; often even with lack of continuity and some backsliding, they have had a kind of ratchet effect. (2) although it is easy to theorize, especially in a time of scarce

ODA, about the possibility of sage policy influence inciting indigenous reforms that reduce the need for aid, transfers and effective reforms in fact more often prove to be complements than substitutes—at least in the near term, as the reforms are taking hold.

Like aid everywhere, there are plenty of flaws and failures in the Asian aid record. Moreover, in per capita terms, the flow of concessional resources to Asia has been thin. It can by no means be the principal explanation for the strong growth and development records that many Asian countries have made since mid-century. And yet, net, with all these reservations plus the political preoccupations that have guided many of the programs much of the time, aid to Asia has on balance indeed "worked."* It has a good project record. It prevented collapses, early in Korea, more recently in Bangladesh. It contributed importantly to major sector achievements (irrigation and water management in Pakistan, the green revolution in India, Pakistan and the Philippines). And not least: it has contributed importantly, if only catalytically, to the formation and strengthening of many of the large number of vital development institutions now scattered across the Asian landscape.

* * * * *

The pity is that the outlook for ODA to Asia—if not to the neediest countries such as Bangladesh and Nepal, to the low-income giants as well as Pakistan, Sri Lanka and Indonesia—is now so bleak. The claim that, on the supply side, the cupboard is bare is, in a sense, a canard: U.S. ODA is such a small slice of the federal budget—it is no more than 3 percent of the defense budget—that it lies entirely within the competence of executive and legislative leadership to double our ODA total simply via minor budgetary reallocations. Indeed, it is an easy case that such reallocation would strengthen American national security, not just be appropriate in a broader foreign policy sense.

But there is little real prospect of such a change during the balance of the present administration, either via a straight budget and appropriations route, or via the technically feasible alternative of a one-shot issuance of the IMF's Special Drawing Rights (SDRs) that OECD member countries receiving them would agree to contribute to an augmented IDA (The World Bank's concessional lending program).

Meanwhile, while concerned Americans wonder how they can encourage both the next administration and the U.S. Congress to adopt a more positive view of the uses of development-bent ODA,

*The reference is to the volume by Robert Cassen, *Does Aid Work?* (Oxford, 1986) prepared for the Task Force on Concessional Flows mentioned earlier.

there is a major opportunity for Japan to step into a more central role in the supply of ODA, especially via the multilateral channels of the World Bank and the Asian Development Bank, to the third world generally but, in particular, to low income Asia.

At the same time concern over ODA tasks that remain unfinished should not deflect attention from the fact, not only that all Asian aid recipients seek to end their dependency on ODA before long, but that some, such as Korea, already have done so and others are well on the way. The rate at which these countries "graduate" will depend heavily on their openness to constructive direct foreign investments, on the skill with which they promote their exports, and on their access to OECD and other external markets.

I. Introduction

The term "foreign aid" covers a greater variety of transnational transfers of resources than I shall be treating in this paper. It can be applied to military assistance; to transfers, as in the Marshall Plan, from an economically developed country to other developed countries; and, in some usages, even to transfers that are nonconcessional, that is, that move on commercial or commercial-like terms that include no element of gift or grant. But my subject is development assistance: This *is* concessional—it has a grant element of at least minimum size; it is economic, not military, assistance; and it goes only to developing countries. Further, I shall be focusing on *official* development assistance (ODA), which is provided by governments or by multilateral agencies that are creatures of governments.

More precisely, my subject is development assistance in Asia. Automatically such a discussion has a time frame, for ODA, whether in Asia or elsewhere, is essentially a post-World War II phenomenon. Overall this postwar period has been one of striking economic development in developing Asia. The coincidence of Asia's development record with this new kind of prodevelopment foreign aid clearly poses a cause-and-effect question. Scarcely anyone who knows the story would call aid the prime mover of Asian development since 1950. But many do assign it a significant, nontrivial, mainly positive role. Conversely, others not only deny such claims; they argue that aid more often than not has retarded development.

The reality that these conflicting views address is complex. Aid comes from so many sources in so many forms with so many particular motives and objects, into such widely varying environments (as these are set both by external conditions and by recipient country policies) and it is subject to such a variety of implementation or managerial modes on the sides of both recipients and donors that its effects nearly defy crisp summary. Morever, just as there is no single, scientific, open-and-shut answer to what aid has accomplished overall in Asia, there can be no certainty about its future.

These are questions, however, of obvious policy interest, and I shall try to respond to them. The answers that can be given are imprecise. But they are not weak. By now there is a burden of evidence and analysis that permits a robust set of judgments about the role of development aid in Asia.

In laying ground for this assessment it is necessary, first, to write at some length about the nature of development assistance in general. In recent years there has been much concern within the development promotion community, not only about the comparative need for aid in different regions and subregions of the third world, but about the past, present and future effectiveness of aid in achieving its main purposes.

This issue is reviewed broadly and then, in the central portion of the paper, with specific reference to Asia. In the latter case the array of donors, the array of recipients and the scale of the concessional flows from one to the other are identified. Thereafter the analysis dwells on the evolution of particular country programs, looking at their varied rationales and effects, including the interplay between the two main *commodities*—(1) resource transfers and (2) influences on policy—that aid supplies.

Finally, having examined the mismatch between development aid's predominantly good record in Asia and its bleak prospects for support in the next years ahead, I speculate about possible scenarios for relaxing the constraints.

II. Development Assistance in General

The Nature of ODA

As indicated, development aid consists of resource transfers. The bulk of these, if one is quantifying aid in conventional dollar-volume terms, are capital transfers: the recipient gets foreign exchange—if he is very lucky, free foreign exchange, more typically foreign exchange with uses restricted to certain sources (e.g., suppliers in the donor country) or to certain forms (e.g., commodities declared to be eligible for procurement) or certain purposes, as in the case of project assistance. Or the capital can be provided in kind: the recipient receives commodities directly instead of being given the money with which to go into the international market and buy them. However, these various forms of capital assistance all can be expressed as financial transfers—which is why a paper on the role of ODA in Asia belongs in a collection on financing Asian development.

Looked at as a program conducted jointly by a set of donor and recipient institutions, aid consists of more than financial flows. Some of its most important components may not, compared with big capital assistance, add up to very much in dollar terms; these are various forms of technical cooperation that help build human capital in recipient countries and assist the latter in acquiring, adapting and developing technology and expertise. Aid transactions also may enhance subsequent trade between countries and encourage private capital flows. Aid can involve a discussion and dialogue between donors and recipients that may exert significant influences (frequently but not invariably benign) on recipient policies. Nevertheless, although in this review I will have occasion to touch on all these dimensions of ODA, the emphasis will be on the financial dimension.

Concessionality—a grant or gift element—is an essential aspect of the definition of official development assistance. OECD's Development Assistance Committee (DAC) established the convention nearly twenty years ago: to qualify as ODA, a transfer must have a grant element of at least 25 percent, the size of this element being determined by the duration of the loan, the grace period, and the extent to which the interest rate charged by the donor is lower than the market rate.[1] Grant elements can run as high as 100 percent—as they do in the case of outright grants. International Development Association (IDA) credits from the soft loan side of the World Bank have carried a grant element of 86 percent, and all the ODA, bilateral and multilateral, now provided by DAC governments has an average grant element of more than 90 percent.

A grant, of course, is a gift, and why some nation states give gifts to other nation states is, on a moment's reflection, puzzling. The business of a national government, particularly a democratic government that is the servant of its citizens-voters-taxpayers, is to advance the interests of its constituents, not to give charity to outsiders. Thus a certain fuzziness typically surrounds the purposes of aid. Countries receiving unrequited transfers often suspect the donors of self-serving motives—and, in fact, the donors commonly are disposed, in terms of their domestic politics, to explain what they are doing in self-serving (i.e., national-interest-serving) terms.

Purposes and Motives

In the international arena, the official position of donor countries always is that they give economic assistance to third world countries for the purpose of promoting the development of the latter. Indeed, under the doctrines of DAC, the traditional donors certify as much by reporting their concessional transfers as development assistance. Moreover, these same donor countries have joined others in forming and funding multilateral agencies, such as the World Bank, the regional development banks, and the United Nations Development Program (UNDP), that dispense multilateral ODA. The member governments of these multilaterals have mandated the agencies to make development promotion their single-track purpose, something the multilaterals come fairly close to doing, albeit sometimes in a politically contentious environment as well as in a context often conflicted over the nature of development diagnoses and prescriptions and the quality of program implementation.

But the motivation of bilateral aid programs is more complex. Year in and year out most of the actions of a donor government must be driven by its perceptions of its own national interest. In the bilateral setting, therefore, development promotion tends to be an instrumental objective—it is a means for advancing the donor's basic purposes. The donor, typically, has a number of the latter on which development promotion may bear. A few donors may be motivated for extended periods by genuine humanitarianism; their publics do want them to act as surrogates for private philanthropy and to project that national image. On occasions of famines or disasters, for example, most official donors engage in episodes of straightforward humanitarian behavior. But more often the bilaterals are actuated by a variety of other purposes—by geostrategic considerations, particularly in the case of the great powers; by the need to obtain base rights and the like in support of geostrategic designs; by other political or historical ties such as in the case of the ex-colonial powers; and by commercial considerations—to expand exports, to obtain assured or advantageous access to scarce materials, or to open ways for overseas investors.

There is nothing intrinsically bad about these other purposes, and at times it may be possible to pursue one or another of them with maximum, or at least with great, development benefit. Killing two birds with one stone sometimes is feasible. Indeed, in many Asian countries assistance motivated mainly by other purposes has had great development benefits.

Nevertheless, it would be silly to deny that the diverse purposes of aid often dilute or interfere with its development-promoting effectiveness. The most diluting effect is on the intercountry allocation of aid. Aggregate ODA is always in short supply. If one were simply interested in maximizing development one would allocate aid mainly to those countries and groups—the poorest ones—who need development most, weighing in also (a) the extent to which they have demonstrated they can use resources effectively and (b) their comparative lack of creditworthiness. (The theory of the last is simply that those who have better access to commercial loans they can service should, as to ODA, give precedence to other poor countries that are less creditworthy.) But political and other considerations have radically distorted ODA distribution away from such norms. This is why, when donors' allocations for 1982 and 1983 are averaged, 44 percent of direct ODA went to middle income developing countries and only the balance to the low-income countries, despite the fact that the latter not only were worse off but had twice as many people.

Other-than-development purposes have additional distorting effects on aid performance and effectiveness. Commercial self-interest sometimes causes donors to push technologies, processes and priorities that are ill-suited to recipient needs. Similarly, distracting concerns, whether these involve the retention of base rights, matters of geopolitical solidarity or the interests of home-country investors, may cause a donor to mute its encouragement of needed policy reforms by the recipient.

It is for all of these reasons that in recent years those concerned with the promotion of development have been noting that, in an increasingly interdependent world, there is a rationale for development assistance that is self-serving but also unswerving in its pro-development thrust. This is the interest that all countries, developed and developing, small and large, have in "global systems maintenance."[2] No one nation state, even the most powerful, can provide unilaterally for an international trading system, for a financial system, a food system, a pattern of global demographics or, among other things, for a set of ecological arrangements that will serve its interest in keeping the planet a tolerably functioning and orderly place. Quite plainly, no such systems maintenance will be possible for long in the absence of substantial and reasonably equitable material advances in all developing regions and in most developing countries.

The Forms of Aid

The various forms that ODA can take are reasonably well known. Most development assistance always has been and continues to be in the form of project grants or loans; it pays for parts of discrete, usually site-specific, increments in productive capacity. Typically these are in part or in whole physical investments, whether in agriculture, infrastructure, industry, health systems improvements or other sectors. But the donor often contributes also to components of training, education, ongoing research or other kinds of institution building and technical assistance needed to make the project work. Donors engage as well in technical assistance not tied to particular capital projects. Traditionally, they paid only for some or all of the foreign exchange costs of the capital and technical assistance projects to which they were contributing. But twenty years ago some began to pay for some of "their" projects' local costs. Similarly, there are occasions—rather more of them in recent years—in which donors shoulder some of the recurrent or running costs of projects to which they have contributed after the projects have come on stream.

When recipients are caught in resource binds, local and recurrent cost-funding guards against the crippling of activities in which donors have taken an interest. But donors are wary of these forms of funding: they may impose the donors' rather than the recipient's priorities too blindly, and they are not conducive to self-help (that is, they may substitute for rather than augment the recipient's saving).

Nonproject aid runs a considerable gamut. The most flexible and discretionary, from the viewpoint of the recipient, is the kind the United States gives Israel. We simply write checks. Equally flexible when appropriate is debt relief. When the creditor government postpones due dates on payments of principal or interest, this frees foreign exchange for whatever other use the debtor government wishes to make of it. Donors can give "balance-of-payment" or "nonproject" loans with no programmatic attribute other than that of plugging a macroeconomic gap; such transfers may, however, be tied as to source and as to the range or categories of commodities for which they can be used. Much the same characteristics inhere in "program" grants or loans, which, as the label indicates, do purport to have specific programmatic purposes (say, underwriting a set of liberalization reforms), or "adjustment" or "sector" loans (the latter assisting adjustment or development in a whole sector or subsector of the recipient economy). Nonproject grants and credits have proven to be better vehicles than project loans for conveying policy influence. Hence the increased interest in "policy-based lending" (e.g., on the part of the World Bank) in recent years has raised the salience of nonproject types of transfers.

Other special forms of aid can be fitted within the foregoing framework. Export credits—if their terms are sufficiently concessional—are classified as ODA. They can be for pieces of projects; or if they are for miscellaneous merchandise, say, for a range of materials and spare parts, they are a form of nonproject lending. But in either case the function of export credits is to help market the donor's exports at terms that make them relatively attractive to the recipient. "Commodity" aid, if one is not simply speaking of a diversified nonproject transfer, is a loan or grant whose applicability is limited to a single or limited type of commodity. The main case is that of food (and certain other agricultural commodities). Most food aid is appropriately classified as a form of nonproject aid; some of it, however, moves as an input to certain projects, such as those involving food for work and target-group nutrition.

Terms: Dimensions of Softness

It has been noted that a loan, according to DAC nomenclature, must have a grant element of at least 25 percent to qualify as ODA. The 1985 DAC chairman's report conveys the meaning of such a 25 percent grant element by illustrating three different combinations of interest rate, loan duration and grace period that would meet this 25 percent grant-element minimum (assuming, as DAC calculations do, that the market interest rate is 10 percent):

—4 percent interest, seven years maturity, including three years' grace
—5 percent interest, eleven years maturity, including four years' grace, or
—5 percent interest, fifteen years maturity, no grace period.[3]

I have already mentioned the high degree of "softness"—the large average grant element—that aid donors are now building into their ODA. This is the one dimension in which most of the donors are exceeding their collective targets. The reason probably is that the aid agencies and ministries in many donor governments are inclined to be more forthcoming than their chief executives or parliaments allow. Being held short of the aid volumes they would prefer, aid administrators find their parliaments comparatively indifferent to whether the country's ODA goes as grants or as only semi-soft loans. Each, in the short run in which parliaments and executives do their decision making, requires the same budgetary appropriation. So, as to financial terms, the administrators opt for the best deals for recipients they can get.

On another aspect of terms, however—the matter of "tying"—bilateral politics are not nearly so permissive. Within the aid policy community it has long been recognized that the quality, i.e., the effectiveness, of ODA is diminished by source tying. When the recipient is denied the option of shopping the world market for aid-funded imports, the value of what he gets per aid dollar tends to be lowered. It has long been recognized that the disadvantage is greater in the case of "double tying"—that is, in cases where the recipient must buy his aid goods from a donor source, and his grant or loan is also tied as to use.[4] For example, if it is a U.S. project loan for a fertilizer factory it must be spent in the United States, and there are only two American suppliers of the type of large centrifugal compressors the project specifies. The source tying of use-tied project loans maximizes the recipient's exposure to oligopolistic pricing.

Recognition of this principle, however, has not moved many bilateral programs away from a norm of source tying during the past fifteen years. At one point in the early 1970s the traditional donors came fairly close to joining in an aid-untying compact, but for many of them the balance-of-payments pressures became prohibitive, and so they have remained. Recipients' spokespersons, for example, in United Nations conferences and in the Task Force on Concessional Flows[5] always demand untying. The matter is debated intermittently within DAC, but without progress. Thus it is that the tying issue adds to the contrast between bilateral and multilateral aid—because the latter (with a few rare exceptions) is essentially untied—and on this count, therefore, of higher quality than tied bilateral aid.

Bilateral and Multilateral Programs

As I will emphasize, virtually all ODA comes from donor governments. Thus the volume of multilateral aid depends on the fraction of their total concessional contribution to development that the donors choose to channel through the multilateral agencies. From the late 1960s to 1983–1984 for the members of DAC, that fraction doubled (from less than 15 percent to a figure of 27 percent, if members' contributions to the EEC's ODA are not treated as multilateral aid, and to a figure of 32 percent if EEC aid is counted on the multilateral side). The rise in the multilateral fraction was substantial and fairly steady until 1979. Since then it has flattened, with some donors throttling back on their multilateral allocations.

In terms of interregional allocations, this slowdown or reversal in multilateral growth is of some concern to Asia. Whereas in the period 1981–1983, 31 percent of the ODA received by all low-income countries worldwide came from multilateral sources (excluding the EEC), 45 percent of the Asian low-income countries' ODA was multilateral. In particular, IDA has supplied a disproportionate share of the comparatively thin flows of ODA going to the two Asian giants, India and China.

Bilateral and multilateral aid each has its advantages. As noted, multilateral aid does better in the matter of tying. The financial terms of bilateral aid are somewhat softer on average. Although there is much variance across the set, bilateral donors give more outright grants. Multilateral aid is more single-mindedly aimed at development promotion, and this shows up, for one thing, in the realm of intercountry allocations. Some bilateral aid—Sweden's is a good example—is heavily concentrated on the low-income countries. But the political considerations motivating the allocations of such donors as the United States, France, Australia and the Arab-OPEC funds and governments cause a much heavier relative flow of aggregate bilateral ODA to middle-income countries than characterizes the multilaterals, especially the soft loan operations of the World Bank and the Asian Development Bank.

In both categories the efficiency of operations varies widely as between different donor agencies. Some of the multilaterals—the World Bank is the outstanding case—have an abundance of highly qualified technical staff who adhere consistently to high analytical and operating standards. Some bilaterals, on the other hand, often have operated more flexibly, have demonstrated quicker reflexes in responding to unexpected needs, and have been more innovative in their program experimentation.

The well-advertised slowdown in multilateral aid during the 1980s thus far has occasioned much concern, exhortation and counter-exhortation. It is quite clear that the relationship between the two modes is not an either-or one. Both are going to be with us for the foreseeable future. It is important that they work in harmony rather than at cross purposes.

Sources of Concessionality

The point to be made here is simple, but it deserves underscoring. The grant element that makes concessional assistance concessional cannot come from a commercial source. Private philanthropies, of course, can provide private grants, but nearly all public grant elements come directly or indirectly from taxpayers. Since the power to tax is jealously guarded by national and subnational parliaments, this means that parliamentary appropriations are the origin of virtually all ODA. There are some small exceptions: the multilateral development banks make relatively modest profits, some of which they channel directly into multilateral ODA. Moreover, when multilateral soft loans are repaid, the lending agency may recycle the proceeds into fresh ODA grants or loans without further reference to donor governments. The same can be said of bilateral loan reflows if the donor government's parliamentary practices permit. When the IMF sold some of its gold holdings in the 1970s, some of the proceeds served as ODA, and now *they* are being recycled into further soft loans. But all these exceptions together account for only a few percentage points of the total ODA flow. All the rest comes from current national budgetary appropriations.

Such will continue to be the case as long as national governments retain their near monopoly on the power to tax (and to run budgetary deficits). The Brandt Commission, for example, has proposed that the United Nations or one of its constituent components be empowered to levy a tax directly on some such base as international trade or international air travel without the intervention of national governments.[6] But so far the doctrine of national sovereignty has not given such suggestions the time of day. So far the idea that a supranational authority might generate resources out of extranational portions of the global commons, such as the seabed, has been equally unavailing. Indeed, to date we have not even managed to convert into development assistance a portion of the "paper gold"—the special drawing rights—that the IMF from time to time creates to augment the world's supply of international liquidity, despite the fact that technically this would be quite feasible.

It is important, therefore, for aid realists to retain a straight and narrow view of the instrument's source. People impatient with the niggardliness of national governments spend a great deal of time speculating about new and exotic (i.e., nonappropriated) sources of aid with a high measure of "automaticity." A fresh study along these lines was contributed to the work of the 1982–1985 Task Force on Concessional Flows by its Nordic and Dutch members.[7] But like other examinations that had preceded it, it found little of near-or medium-term promise in such possibilities. The same conservative judgment must be rendered about various schemes for "stretching" ODA—blending it with nonconcessional market funds or using it to subsidize the interest rates on funds borrowed in the market. Such measures are mechanically feasible, but they cannot manufacture concessionality. They may repackage what there is of the latter, but, as things now stand, only donor governments will continue to create it.

Recent Concerns and Reviews

By now development assistance has a history of nearly forty years, but it has not yet become an accepted part of the landscape. In some donor countries aid programs and agencies have been through a series of temporary incarnations; the activity was not expected to endure for very long. As it was renewed in one parliamentary battle after another, too many promises were made to various constituencies. Expectations were inflated, particularly in the aftermath of the Marshall Plan's quick and fundamentally different success. Meanwhile, not only has development (despite its impressive statistical averages) been proving a fundamentally difficult, often tedious, process; development assistance, reaching through and around the sovereign sensitivities of one nation state into those of another, has proven to be fundamentally awkward. Usually it has been too small an input to dominate outcomes—but not too small to be blamed for failures.

Perhaps because of underlying skepticism about the appropriateness of ongoing public transfers to other countries, perhaps simply because aid has such a thin and limited internal constituency, aid's worth and effectiveness are challenged far more than are domestic programs being conducted with no greater efficiency. Such questioning and criticism pick up whenever resource constraints tighten, and they have been in full voice for the better part of a decade now. This is clearly not the first time that observers have detected "aid fatigue." A week before John Kennedy was killed he told a press conference, with regard to congressional resistance to aid authorizations, "I don't understand why we are suddenly so fatigued." Nor is this the first time that, along with stepped up media attention, the worthwhileness of aid has been the subject of official reappraisals. But the number and breadth of the latter have been unusual in recent years, and it is useful for our purposes to take note of at least two of them. Both, to be sure, can be assumed to be biased, since they were conducted by participants in the ODA enterprise. Each of them, however, has sought to provide a balanced assessment, and together they offer substantial testimony as to the net value of aid.

The first was a special project of the largest ongoing aid-monitoring effort, namely, that conducted by the seventeen member countries and the secretariat of the OECD's Development Assistance Committee in Paris. At the end of 1985, Rutherford M. Poats, then chairman of DAC, chose to cast the chairman's annual report, *Development Cooperation*, into a review of twenty-five years of aid on DAC's silver anniversary.[8] Nine chapters of the report are devoted to long-term trends in aid and other international resource flows, four chapters to "the continuing efforts to make aid more effective" and three to an appraisal of the twenty-five year record.

The first of these final chapters of the DAC volume, after nicely sketching the way the debate over aid effectiveness has unfolded since the late 1970s, summarizes the findings of the growing accumulation of project evaluations that are made by the World Bank, by some other multilaterals including the EEC, and increasingly by DAC member aid agencies. In these project-evaluation programs there is a rough convergence on the conclusion that about a third of aid's capital projects are highly successful; a third "can be judged satisfactory"; and a final third are disappointing. Of these last, about 10 percent of the total have to be regarded as "a total loss." The report surmises that such a record compares favorably with the performance of both domestic governmental projects and overseas private investments.

The DAC report dwells on a point that virtually all informed recent assessments of aid have emphasized, namely that during the past generation practitioners of aid, both donors and recipients, have been going through a massive learning experience. Thus effectiveness can be and is on the rise. Then, in the following chapter, the report goes on to consider ODA's macroeconomic record. This, the authors rightly emphasize, is a much more difficult question because of the problem of multiple causes: more often than not, aid is a lesser determinant of outcomes. Moreover, much of it is deliberately concentrated on countries with the worst development problems; it should not be surprising that it does not have a good correlation with good growth and equity performance. And yet, says DAC, a number of the more heavily aided countries—Botswana, Jordan, Taiwan, Korea, Tunisia, Indonesia, Ivory Coast and Pakistan—have had some of the better growth records.

The other large-scale review exercise, to which the 1985 DAC report draws attention, was the Task Force on Concessional Flows launched in 1982 by the Development Committee, which comprises developed and developing country ministers, mostly of finance, and is jointly attached to the World Bank and the IMF. The Development Committee from time to time has used the device of assigning a task force composed of senior officials of an agreed group of its member countries to report on a particular issue in a time-bound fashion. In this case, those countries that style themselves "like-minded" (the four Nordic countries, the Netherlands and Canada) were discouraged in the early 1980s by the reluctance of some donors—especially the largest, the United States—to increase their ODA. The members of the "like-minded" group were mindful of the widespread skepticism about the effectiveness of aid, and they noted the apparently wide differences in the degrees to which the publics and parliaments of different donor countries supported their governments' development assistance efforts. So these six countries persuaded the Development Committee to establish a Task Force on Concessional Flows with terms of reference requiring it to address aid volume, aid effectiveness and public support for aid.

What mainly distinguished the Task Force from the continuing deliberations of DAC was that the former was a joint forum for aid donors and *recipients*. Eighteen governments agreed to participate, nine members of DAC and nine from the "South"—two Arab/OPEC donors (Saudi Arabia and Kuwait) and seven aid recipients. Among the latter, Asia was well represented by its three most populous aid recipients, China, India and Indonesia. These were joined by Tanzania, Senegal, the Dominican Republic and Costa Rica. On the side of the traditional donors, the "big five" (the United States, Japan, Germany, France and the United Kingdom) participated along with three from the sponsoring group (Canada, the Netherlands and Finland acting for the four Nordics); Italy and Belgium shared the ninth chair. The World Bank staffed the Task Force, and the writer was recruited as an independent chairman.

After eight multiday meetings and a great deal of input by the staff, by member government agencies and by consultants, the Task Force presented its final report to the Development Committee in October 1985.[9] From the beginning the group saw that its three subjects were closely linked. In the end, having deliberated the longest over it, it addressed the matter of aid effectiveness first.

Here, recognizing the pervasiveness of the skepticism and therefore the usefulness of an arm's-length assessment, the Task Force hired a dozen consultants—seasoned specialists in aid operations and analysis, headed by Professor Robert Cassen of the Institute of Development Studies at the University of Sussex—to make a variety of country studies, project evaluations surveys, technical assistance reviews and other specialized studies that Cassen synthesized into a book-length report entitled *Does Aid Work?*[10] The latter is the most serious piece of "effectiveness literature" yet produced. It assembles project-evaluation results in much the same way as does the 1985 DAC report. It is highly critical of some aspects of the record. It points to country and to broad sector successes and failures; it gives aid higher marks for growth promotion than poverty alleviation, essentially because of the greater difficulty of the latter. In its international comparisons, the report emphasizes the weakness of the record in much of Africa. It dwells on the centrality of recipient policies and urges that, because it is a lesser input but has a catalytic potential, its effects be looked at systemically rather than in isolation. Looking through such lenses, the Cassen group found an overwhelming case for the development-promotion usefulness of aid. And, like the DAC report and like the Task Force itself, which essentially adopted its consultants' analysis of the effectiveness issue, Cassen underscored the learning that has been going on and therefore the ready scope that aid donors, aid recipients and the two acting jointly have for increasing the efficiency and impact of their operations.

On the subject of the public support for aid, the Task Force remarked on the great differences among the "aid politics" that characterize different donor countries and, indeed, that can appear over time in the same country. However, the Task Force reviewed some recent survey research seeming to indicate current similarities in public attitudes in several DAC donor countries: publics lack enthusiasm for development assistance but have little entrenched or high-priority hostility toward it. Instead—and this was the Task Force's strongest judgment on the second of its three broad subjects—the most important determinant of public support for aid, and the factor most likely to shift public and parliamentary attitudes toward development-promotion policy from a negative to a positive mode, is executive leadership. Within limits, more often than not, a prime minister or president can get as much ODA as he or she is prepared (politically) to pay for. Having said this, the Task Force also recognized the obvious and strong dependency that support for aid has on *perceptions* of aid effectiveness, and therefore on seeing, not only that aid operations are effective, but that this becomes widely known.

Initiators of the Task Force had aid volume most clearly in mind, and in the end it was that subject that occasioned the most interesting and extensive convergence of views among Task Force members. Early in the proceedings it sounded as if the United States, spokesman for the most restrained donor viewpoint, and India, the most articulate recipient member, could never agree on volume. But in the end complete agreement—between these two and indeed among all eighteen members—developed along the following lines.

First (without questioning the desirability of greater self-reliance), there is a need for substantially increased ODA. But present prospects are that ODA supplies during the balance of the 1980s will slow down to only about 2 percent real growth annually.

Second, given this disparity between needs and availabilities, the initial response should be to cope with it by one or more of the following options, short of increasing volume above its projected path:

a. Increasing the effectiveness of official aid;
b. Changing current country allocations in favor of those with greater development needs;
c. Concentrating those modest aid increments now expected on low-income countries;
d. Blending ODA with "other nonconcessional official flows" in ways that would yield "a higher overall volume of external resources";
e. Supplementing ODA by encouraging more private philan-

thropic flows to developing countries, more ODA contributions from new donors (e.g., those newly graduating to the role of donors, such as South Korea), more earnings from trade or more private investment.

The Task Force went down this list very carefully. It judged that each of these expedients represented a positive potential; it was on the side of the angels. But, particularly in the near and medium term, the potential was very limited. One example: the chances of getting the United States to reallocate to low-income countries much of the economic aid it gives Israel, or France the aid it gives its overseas departments and territories, are probably less than they are for getting each of these donors to increase its aid volume.

The Task Force, therefore concluded that no one of the measures considered above, nor any combination of them, will cope adequately with the challenge of development in the low-income countries. Since there is no escaping the need for predominant reliance on traditional, appropriated concessional assistance, donor governments should exert redoubled efforts to increase the supply of ODA "as a matter of urgency" (p.24).

These deliberations of the Task Force on Concessional Flows had a particular bearing on the role of development assistance in Asia. The position on aid volume just sketched reflected a deliberate and unanimous rejection of a formula that the chairman and the secretary supplied by the World Bank had, most reluctantly, concluded the Task Force would have to adopt: namely, that given the urgency of the needs in Africa, all or nearly all of the ODA receipts of the Asian low-income countries (probably with the exception of Bangladesh and perhaps Nepal) need to be reallocated to Africa.

It is appropriate to quote the Task Force report at some length on this subject:

[T]he issue, in practical terms, is whether there is still scope for transferring ODA from those low-income countries that have been faring relatively well in terms of growth and self-reliance in recent years . . .

[I]t is necessary to recall and reaffirm the basic development criteria used for allocating scarce ODA resources. The primary criterion is poverty, and on this score the low-income countries that have recently had some success have approximately as strong a claim as have the poorest countries, African and others . . . There are, however, two other criteria. According to the criterion of development performance (closely related to so-called absorptive capacity), low-income countries that have recently been performing well have the edge. Counterposed to the performance standard is the criterion of

creditworthiness. Whereas the "good performers" merit ODA as a reward for performance, those countries that lack creditworthiness also require substantial ODA. This is virtually an issue of national survival in such countries as Bangladesh and many in Sub-Saharan Africa . . .

The principal consideration in assessing prospects for further reallocation within the low-income group, however, is that preferences in favor of the poorer, weaker countries already have been at work. During the past fifteen years the per capita aid receipts of the poorest countries in Africa and elsewhere have been relatively high, and those of the better-performing low-income countries have been relatively low. China has only recently started receiving modest amounts of ODA. Since 1970 India's aid share has declined by roughly one-half. African countries now receive about eight times the per capita ODA level going to India and a far greater multiple than the level of China.

The larger low-income countries have shown more impressive investment, savings, and growth performance than have many middle-income countries during this decade . . . We, however, emphasize that these low-income countries are heavily burdened with large populations, a significant proportion of which exist in absolute poverty. Their resources are still much too limited to make the major social investments needed to provide barely acceptable living standards for most of their people. Their continuing efforts to overcome poverty must command sustained support from the development community. Their recent achievements hold out considerable promise for a better future. They have made major and costly efforts in undertaking policy reforms to enhance economic efficiency. These efforts are paying off and need sustained support if the gains are not to be swiftly dissipated.

These large low-income countries have also shown remarkable performance in achieving high domestic savings rates at extremely low per capita income levels. They cannot, therefore, be faulted on the grounds of becoming permanently aid-dependent. At the same time, it is clear that there are considerable risks in imposing a premature restriction on their access to aid. For all these reasons we believe that concessional resource allocations to these large poor countries should be based on their broad economic situation and should not constitute, in effect, a penalty for performance.

This, in turn, provides an appropriate entree to my assigned subject, namely, development assistance in Asia.

III. Development Assistance in Asia—Until Now

The story of aid in Asia should prove to any development purist that development assistance does not always have to be either bountiful or high-minded to be useful. There have been a few Asian cases where clients have been flooded with ODA (Vietnam was the extreme, and least successful, instance), but for the most part aid flows to Asian countries, especially the populous ones, have been quite lean compared, for example, with those to many African and Middle Eastern recipients. The purposes of much of the bilateral ODA, moreover, have been distinctly political. Yet there are many cases in the forty year record—almost surely a predominant number, looking across the array of Asian developing countries—where the prodevelopment effectiveness of aid must be given high marks.

The Scale and Structure of Asian Aid

Development assistance to Asia has been an evolving story. Its purposes have been varied and sometimes blurred. The leading actor on the donor side has been the United States, but it has had various roles, and they have been diminishing. The shifting balances between bilateral and multilateral sources have been different for different recipients. Indeed the development aid experience can be best reviewed recipient country by recipient country, and that—focusing far more on some countries than others—is what I undertake to do in much of what follows.

But, first, readers may, as it were, wish to scan the Asian aid scene through a wide angle lens. Table 1 provides a broad and summary quantification of the activity that, selectively, will be traced chronologically in subsequent sections of the paper. It extends from 1971, the earliest year for which consistent published country estimates are available, to 1983. This time span misses the earlier parts of the story covered below, and it does not bring matters down to date to the extent the conclusion of the paper will do. But these are not serious deficiencies since the function of the table is cross-sectional, it covers enough of Asia's ODA history to illustrate the overall scale of aid and its distributional structure. It also offers a framework for recording some brief country-by-country notes on aid sources that can be provided for all of the listed countries. In subsequent sections of the paper, I turn to more detailed and selective country chronologies.

In Table 1 OECD's estimates for countries' net receipts of aid have been converted into constant dollars. It becomes apparent that aggre-

Table 1
Net Disbursements of Bilateral and Multilateral Official Development Assistance to Northeast and Southeast Asia and to South Asian Countries
1971 through 1983 (in 1982 dollars)
(millions of dollars)

	1971	1972	1973	1974	1975	1976	1977	1978	1979	1980	1981	1982	1983
Northeast and Southeast Asia:													
Northeast Asia NICs													
Republic of Korea	732	787	570	467	422	345	352	227	170	162	352	34	8
Taiwan	23	13	−53	−33	−34	−33	25	8	25	−5	9	−6	8
China	—	—	—	—	—	—	—	—	17	66	507	524	608
Southeast Asia													
Indochina(1)	1300	1529	1416	1998	806	342	416	614	641	643	433	218	167
Indonesia	1327	1082	1244	1228	1167	1060	767	880	917	1109	1037	906	716
Malaysia/Singapore	194	189	164	215	295	187	191	171	214	219	201	183	247
Philippines	164	353	451	294	304	296	272	345	340	355	400	333	408
Thailand	142	116	123	133	147	268	198	360	499	488	432	389	413
Total	3882	4069	3915	4302	3107	2465	2221	2605	2823	3037	3371	2581	2580
South Asia													
Bangladesh	34	482	853	967	1717	843	1137	1371	1471	1473	1165	1347	1032
India	2259	1320	1576	2515	2882	2886	1643	1855	1771	2482	2037	1550	1655
Pakistan	932	656	572	1287	1504	2024	811	928	794	1214	865	902	693
Sri Lanka	126	125	117	150	295	263	278	449	408	459	399	416	452
Other(2)	372	396	384	341	339	393	428	630	821	619	545	548	519
Total	3723	2979	3502	5260	6737	6409	4297	5233	5265	6247	5011	4763	4351

Notes: 1) Includes Vietnam, Laos and Cambodia. 2) Principally Nepal, Burma, Afghanistan, Maldives and Bhutan.
Source: Organization for Economic Cooperation and Development and (for U.S. GNP deflator) U.S. Department of Commerce.

gated aid flows to Asia (the table does not include West Asian countries) were not in a growth mode during the 1970s and early 1980s. In Northeast and Southeast Asia the annual growth rate in real ODA during the dozen years 1971–1983 was a negative 3.4 percent; leave out the bulge in U.S. aid to Vietnam in the early years of the period and real ODA still declined 1.7 percent annually. In South Asia there was a positive real growth but of very modest proportions: 1.3 percent annually, essentially concentrated in the two countries of Bangladesh and Sri Lanka. The combined regions of South Asia and Northeast and Southeast Asia experienced a nearly flat real aid flow during this period; real net concessional receipts declined at an annual rate of 0.8 percent. The period, moreover, was one during which collective real national incomes in the OECD countries rose slowly but significantly. Thus, as a fraction of GNP, ODA to the parts of Asia under review here fell by roughly one quarter.

Now for the brief country-by-country comments that this panoramic view of Asian aid invites: The two newly-industrializing countries in Northeast Asia at the top of the table were already in an aid graduation or post-graduation phase in the 1970s. Previously the two principal bilateral donors to both countries had been the United States and Japan. Both were cutting back in Korea during the 1970s; both already were receiving net repayments of principal from Taiwan at that time. And, as to concessional transfers, the principal multilateral donors (the World Bank and the Asian Development Bank) also essentially had tuned out by 1980, finding both Taiwan and Korea readily capable of borrowing at market terms.

The Philippines and Thailand are two ASEAN countries that have the same 50–million-person size as South Korea but with per-capita incomes—lower than Korea's—in the same middle range. Although the two countries' political and economic experiences have differed greatly in recent years, their quantitative aid histories have been similar. In the late 1970s and early 1980s, despite more urgent needs in Africa and South Asia, real aid flows to Thailand and the Philippines were pumped up quite considerably for predominantly regional reasons. Earlier the United States had been the chief bilateral donor to both countries and especially to the Philippines. But near the end of the 1970s Japan began rapidly to raise its overall aid effort. However—like France or Belgium, unlike the United States and West Germany—Japan had (and still has) a strong geographic gradient in its aid allocations. It tends to be more generous with countries in its own regional neighborhood. Hence the boost for Thailand and the Philippines, which also was commercially advantageous to Japanese exporters and direct investors.

Japan has played the same leading role in Indonesia, accounting, during the period covered by Table 1, for 30 percent of all ODA and 36 percent of DAC bilateral ODA to that country. Indonesia has had a fairly attentive consortium of aid donors chaired by its former colonial power, the Netherlands; and in the early 1970s the country, with three times the population of either the Philippines or Thailand, received more than three times the aid going to either one. Thus—perhaps because Indonesia was poor (real income per capita was a third lower than the average for the other two countries)—it seemed to defy the generalization that large countries are relatively less successful than small ones in attracting ODA. But then the two oil shocks (of 1974 and 1979) and Indonesia's membership in OPEC probably dampened the country's aid receipts moderately: it was and still is poor, but most of the intervening years it has had enhanced access to foreign exchange.

Aid to the countries of Indochina—three fifths or more of it went to Vietnam, the rest to Laos and Kampuchea during the period covered by the table—had two phases. The heavy years through 1975 were overwhelmingly an American affair. Thereafter U.S. ODA stopped entirely, and a different collection of DAC, OPEC and multilateral donors (the leading DAC donor during this phase was Sweden) maintained a lower but nontrivial ODA flow, over and above Vietnam's receipts of Soviet assistance, which the table does not cover.

It was remarked that the division of labor between bilateral and multilateral ODA has varied greatly among Asian countries. The following, in ascending order, were, for the last three years covered in Table 1, the fractions of total ODA received from multilateral sources:

The Philippines	*.15*	*Bangladesh*	*.33*
Indonesia	*.16*	*Pakistan*	*.44*
Sri Lanka	*.26*	*Indochina*	*.50*
Thailand	*.28*	*India*	*.65*

India's exceptional dependence on multilateral aid in part reflects the fact that multilateral aid agencies as a group, and the World Bank in particular, are less prone than most bilateral donors to the country-is-a-country syndrome in formulating their aid allocations. Thus they discriminate less against the populous—especially against the poor populous—countries. But in addition there is an element of history in the Indian case. During the 1960s the United States was much the largest donor to India. During the first year in Table 1, 1971—the last in which that pattern prevailed—relations between India and the United States were nearly fractured in the course of Bangladesh's separation from Pakistan. Thereupon bilateral American aid to India was radically reduced and, under an arrangement agreeable to both countries, IDA stepped into the role of lead donor. Since then, as has been seen already and will be discussed further below, the volume of aid to India has been a function, in good part, of (a) the overall availability of resources for IDA and (b) the competing claims of other poor countries on those resources.

Bangladesh is the large South Asian country case in which, because of the depth and breadth of its poverty, the bilateral donors have remained most active. The United States has been the leading bilateral donor, but it has been topped in some years by Japan while a number of other DAC members, including Canada, Germany and the United Kingdom, have been major contributors. At the same time, the Asian Development Bank and UNDP have provided considerable assistance, and inputs from IDA, the heaviest of the multilateral donors, have approximately paralleled those from the United States.

Pakistan, being roughly analogous to India economically but, since its separation from Bangladesh, only one eighth the size, always has received far more ODA per capita than its neighbor. As between Pakistan and Bangladesh, the latter was the more populous and the one that the traditional donors previously had neglected but had come to favor since partition because of its greater poverty and perhaps because of the circumstance of its formation. During the mid–1970s, however, the dampening effect of all of this on ODA to Pakistan was more than offset by the generosity of the newly affluent OPEC donors. During this period the latter provided concessional transfers to a number of other Asian countries but none to rival those to Pakistan.

The last country line in Table 1 that invites comment is that for Sri Lanka. The fact that the annual growth rate in real ODA to Sri Lanka (about 11 percent) was the highest during 1971–1983 among all the countries listed partly reflects donor approval of the changes in economic policy that accompanied Sri Lanka's regime changes in the 1970s. But the record may demonstrate even more (especially under conditions of aid management by aid consortia) the greater scope for converting surges in donor sentiment into swings in aid volume that inheres in small country cases.

Some Early Happenstances

It is easy in retrospect to impose rational patterns on sequences of happenings that in fact were less tidy and more accidental. Thus, like other writers, I have been inclined to say that U.S. *development* assistance started with President Truman's Point IV (technical assistance) speech in 1949, and that this American initiative, if one discounts the colonial predecessors of various subsequent European efforts, was the first of its kind. But in fact from the moment World War II ended, the United States was heavily engaged in activities in East Asia whose content, problems and resource requirements were indistinguishable from what would become development assistance. The United States was heavily engaged in rebuilding and building the Japanese economy and promoting all manner of institutional reforms in that country. It ran a military government from mid–1945 to August 1948 in South Korea, spent some $300 million doing so, put in another $100 million of Economic Cooperation Administration (Marshall Plan) money *and* pushed through a thorough land reform, as it was doing in Japan itself. For that matter, the United States had a brief innings with an ECA program for the Kuomingtang government in China until the Communists prevailed in 1949. In another ad hoc operation, the U.S. Export-Import Bank acted as the government's agent for an emergency wheat loan of $190 million to India in 1951. All of this happened before President Truman's 1949 Point IV scheme had been translated into legislation and activated by means of such technical assistance agreements as the one negotiated with India in January 1952.

There is a further oddity about the early American development assistance record. If one examines Gordon Gray's report to the president on foreign economic policies of November 1950[11] and the March 1951 report of the U.S. International Development Advisory Board, headed by Nelson Rockefeller[12] it becomes clear that the Truman administration was disposed to provide capital loans and grants through multilateral rather than bilateral channels. Whereas a UN committee of experts, including Arthur Lewis, Theodore Schultz and D.R. Gadgil of India, recommended in the spring of 1951 that $1 billion of loan money be transferred to developing countries annually mainly by the IBRD, partly by the U.S. Export-Import Bank, the Gray report a few months earlier had recommended the same pattern on a scale of $600–800 million. Moreover, in March 1951 the Rockefeller report agreed with the forthcoming UN document that there should be a substantial annual provision of concessional funds by a multilateral body for public non-self-liquidating infrastructure. Quantitatively, U.S. thinking on the last was not as ambitious as that of the United Nations experts, and the United States preferred that the facility (what eventually became IDA) be governed under the World Bank (dollar-weighted) rather than a UN (one flag, one vote) voting scheme. But big prodevelopment aid was to be multilateral; bilateral development assistance was to be confined, Point IV style, mainly to technical assistance and food aid.

This was a case, however, in which policy theory was overridden by faits accomplis in Taiwan and Korea. In Taiwan the friendly refugee government of the Republic of China urgently required substantial support that the United States felt obligated to supply without waiting for multilateral processing. In Korea it turned out that the requirements were greater than could be accommodated within the available multilateral framework. As the Korean War was winding down in 1952–1953, the UN Korean Reconstruction Agency (UNKRA), which, under a formula of 66 percent U.S. funding and 34 percent from others, had been established to help put postwar Korea back on its feet and employed Robert R. Nathan Associates of Washington, D.C. to analyze the country's reconstruction and development needs. In 1953 an overlapping U.S. government study was made by a team headed by economic diplomat Henry Tasca. The findings of the two studies surprised many people at the time; the scale of the country's external resource requirements was quite beyond the capacity of UNKRA, because there was no way that 34 percent of the requirements could be raised from non-U.S. sources. The United States under what it perceived as geopolitical compulsion, would have to go it alone. Thus, contrary to what had been its emerging development assistance theory, the United States backed into major bilateral capital programs in East Asia, and thereafter this pattern became the American norm.

Donor Purposes—Mostly American

It is not quite right, in reviewing the beginnings of development assistance to Asia, to discuss only U.S. programs. The French, of course, were still involved in Indochina, and there was a postcolonial follow-up in the case of the British: the Commonwealth initiated the Colombo Plan (the Council for Technical Cooperation in South and South East Asia) in 1950, which the United States joined in 1951, Japan in 1954. Nevertheless the thrust of these Asian aid beginnings was overwhelmingly American as well as bilateral.

The inaugural pattern was complex in the mixture of purposes displayed. The Colombo Plan, with India, Pakistan and the then Ceylon among its original signatories, was presumably aimed at development as an end in itself. So, as the record is usually read, was the United States' own technical cooperation initiative, Point IV. In those days (we may have come full circle) there may have been nothing the United States did in the foreign policy realm that completely lacked a cold war echo; but for most, Point IV represented a commitment to the worth of the world's leading nation and leading democracy trying to do good (without massive budgetary implications) to many of the world's poor and emerging nations. Before Point IV was off the ground, however, it was overtaken in June 1950 by the Korean War, whereupon all U.S. foreign policy thinking snapped back into a comparatively militant East-West idiom. The U.S. aid agency was transformed into the Mutual Security Agency (the Point IV administration being folded in), which became heavily preoccupied with matters of defense support, not only in Korea and Taiwan but in Thailand, the Philippines, Vietnam, Pakistan and beyond.

Yet there is a common perception that in a few countries—notably India, where, the Wheat Loan having preceded them by a few months, the technical cooperation program and field mission dated from the beginning of 1952—the American assistance effort continued mainly to be development driven. This, I think, was in fact the case, not only in India but probably also in Sri Lanka and perhaps even in Nepal and Afghanistan. But how could this have been, especially in the era of John Foster Dulles, who said that neutrality (nonalignment) in the East-West struggle was inherently immoral? There are two overlapping explanations.

First, even when looked at from the top down, governments—and most certainly the U.S. government, even when so dominant a figure as Dulles is in place—are never monoliths. They always must pursue multiple objectives, even a variety of foreign policy objectives, simultaneously. And these by no means are always consistent. There was nothing unusual about a mixture of goals being sought within the same administrative frame, or about different country programs within that frame being launched with different dominant purposes.

But there was also a further aid-specific, bottom-up explanation, which some would say concerns the pathologies of bureaucracies. This has to do with the fact that once a number of able, strong, technical and other staff are recruited and placed in the field and they get interested in their work, they become a very considerable party-in-interest for the prosecution of their programs. Not only do they often become skillful, whether by going through channels or out of channels, at injecting their voice into central decision making; there is enough inertia in budgetary and other bureaucratic and legislative processes to make them quite effective.

This is the sort of thing that happened in India, as it were, in spite of John Foster Dulles. The U.S. effort got an initial charismatic push from Chester Bowles in his first incarnation as ambassador. But he tended to overpromise, given the realities in Washington, and he was gone by the start of 1953. The program was carried forward, growing incrementally, on dedicated technocratic momentum. Food aid became associated, motivated initially by surplus-disposal interest on the American side. And then in 1958, with Undersecretary of State Douglas Dillon giving new salience to the U.S. interest in the success of Indian development, the era of large, regularized, capital transfers began in response to the foreign exchange crisis that befell India's Second-Five Year Plan. The U.S. Export-Import Bank opened a $150 million line of credit, Dillon and Eugene Black, president of the World Bank, launched the donor collective (Canada, Germany, Japan, the United Kingdom, the United States and the World Bank) that became Aid-to-India Consortium, and Washington committed itself to major continuing bilateral concessional lending by establishing the Development Loan Fund with India as its first leading client.

It can be argued that in popular thinking about the role of aid in Asian development, India has received too much attention—not only because of its size but because of its head start in terms of a formal, self-initiated, planned development effort. India's absolute amounts of economic aid received since 1950 have been the largest in Asia, and aid, as I shall be saying, has played a significant role in that country. But, quantitatively, aid's real importance, as measured by the country's receipt of ODA per capita, has been lower than in any other continuing Asian aid recipient. (China, following receipt of some Soviet aid in the 1950s, did not start getting ODA again until the end of the 1970s, since when, to be sure, it has had a lower per capita rate than India's.) Moreover, as just argued, the motivation of the largest bilateral donor has not been typical in the case of India. Over the years there has been a great deal of political static—issues concerning Vietnam, votes in the United Nations, and, of course, the Indo-Pakistani rivalry—surrounding the U.S-to-India aid program. But the program's theme plainly was development qua development, until its collapse in 1971–1972 at the time of the Bangladesh War. (Thereafter, as already noted, the United States has expressed its interest in the country more through its support of IDA's large flow of transfers to India than through the token bilateral program that has remained.)

The United States has had a few others of these development qua development cases in Asia: now, beside Nepal and Sri Lanka, also Bangladesh. But the typical U.S. bilateral ODA effort in Asia has been politically motivated—in the leading cases of Taiwan, Korea, the Philippines, Thailand, Indonesia and Pakistan. There have been two such politically motivated cases where the efforts, whatever their mix of purposes, totally failed—Vietnam and Iran. It is fair, however, to leave these two out of this brief review, because it can reasonably be argued that, although development assistance did not forestall the defeat of American interests in either Iran or Vietnam, it also was not responsible for those reversals. Aid was simply swamped by other factors.

This means that the "typical" country case has the following characteristics: the United States has been the leading bilateral donor. It has had a strong political reason for giving its development assistance, but the resources that it has had available for transfer have been subject to fairly tough budgetary rationing. Moreover, the United States is heavily represented on the ground, and its aid mission displays a lively and professional concern for development promotion. There are other bilateral donors, with smaller programs and smaller resident missions, which are not conflicted or in any serious way competitive among themselves or with the United States. But even though the donors are drawn together once a year into a brief consortium or consultative group meeting, their coordination leaves much to be desired. The coordination problem, in one sense, is aggravated by the fact that there are also multilateral actors in this typical Asian country development game: certainly the World Bank from the beginning and its IDA arm after 1960, the Asian Development Bank after 1966, and UNDP and one or another of the UN specialized agencies. In another sense these multilaterals represent a potential for coordination leadership (perhaps most obviously by the World Bank), but it is a potential that has yet to be firmly seized.

As claimed at the outset, this semi-focused aid setup has delivered fairly impressive results in Asia. In the balance of this section I elaborate this view in a series of comments on the actors (donors and the recipients), issues and results of the aid transactions. When not otherwise specified, my references will be to the "typical" country case just sketched. Without attempting thorough country studies, however, we will have occasion to point out contrasts within the majority group. I will also add in development-qua-development cases as appropriate, but will not attempt any comments on China, since the subject is so large and the aid experience so recent.

The Actors: Donor Agencies and Recipient Regimes

The cast conducting development assistance operations in Asia during the past four decades has been of high average competence and seriousness. It has learned from, and not merely accumulated, experience.

The United States has played the central role structuring the Asian development assistance effort and in most countries has involved itself primarily for political reasons. The single factor on the donor side that has contributed most to Asian aid's constructive texture has therefore probably been the professionalism of the officials and technicians of USAID. It is not that USAID's people in the field or headquarters have been consistently brilliant or driven with dedication to their work. But on average they have been able; most of them have worked hard; they have shown some facility at relating to host-country counterparts; and, most important, they and their management have been outstanding in keeping some distance between themselves and their political masters. By this means they have sustained the credibility of their commitment to development. As noted, they also have been numerous on the ground.

AID has been too constantly under congressional, White House, media and interest-group fire, it has been too buffeted by budgetary and regulatory constraints and too embroiled in arguments in the field to develop any inner sense of being an elite, blue-ribbon agency. Indeed, it would be too much to call it that. For one thing, AID loses good people too regularly—many of its best, for example, keep peeling off into more elegant, less bruising jobs in the World Bank. Nevertheless, for the reasons just sketched, it has been a kind of role model for other bilateral aid agencies working in Asia,[13] and it sometimes contributes an augmented knowledge of a country to its multilateral counterparts as well as to its bilateral colleagues.

At the same time, the multilaterals long have played a seasoned role in Asia—the World Bank, of course, from the 1950s onward. By standards of analytical excellence, the World Bank has managed to gather and hold the best development promotion staff, and one of considerable depth. The fact that many of the institution's senior officers and analysts are Asians themselves has contributed to the rapport and influence the Bank has had with regional governments (although one must add that the quality of the Bank's relations with host governments has varied from country to country).

The Asian Development Bank, meanwhile, has established itself as a solid contributor to regional development.[14] In the current decade the Bank has been adopting a more varied and venturesome role as a development promoter. It has been extending its basic lending function beyond project lending to various types of policy-based lending, has been augmenting its technical assistance activity, is doing more private sector promotion, is experimenting with some equity investments, and is becoming a more active networker of regional information and analysis.[15]

One could go on to say positive things about many of the external actors that have been trying to assist Asian development. However, the greatest influencers of the effectiveness of Asian aid have been the recipient governments themselves. During the forty or less years they have been receiving aid, most Asian countries have been served much or most of the time by governments that have been not only strongly but sensibly committed to development. But there has been a great deal of variance, not only between countries but within particular countries from one regime to another.

Thus, whatever one may think of its politics, the government of Taiwan has been an admirable economic development manager straight through.[16] Its donors may have learned from it more than vice versa. Korea under Syngman Rhee, on the other hand, had a contrary, strong-headed, conspicuously corrupt, import-substituting, heavy-industrializing, controls-prone, inflation-bent regime that gave the United States fits for six postwar years as it was pouring in military and economic assistance. Some of this early aid had positive effects. Moreover, the change to the Park regime, which began in 1961, was not a switch from night to day; nor did donor-recipient relations suddenly become and remain congenial. Yet a profound change in Korean economic policies eventually took hold in 1965, and, quickly outdistancing its need for ODA, the Republic of Korea has been setting economic performance records most of the time since.

Indonesia underwent a radical change of regime in the middle 1960s that placed a high premium on economic efficiency, thrust technocrats front and center and has contributed to high growth rates through most of the period since. Unlike Indonesia, Thailand has had a series of regimes and what appears to be a turbulent political record. But there has been a consistent priority for economic development as well as good deal of continuity in generally constructive economic policies. The average growth rate since 1965 has been in the neighborhood of 7 percent, nearly equal to Indonesia's and only moderately below Korea's average annual rate of GDP growth of 8.5 percent for the period 1965–1983. The Philippines has had a significantly slower growth performance (an average rate of 5.4 percent for the same period) by Southeast Asian standards. Until early 1986 the regime had a longevity rivaling its Indonesian counterpart. But as its debt and adjustment problems signaled and as has become clear since the displacement of the Marcos government, the development effort had been in a phase of decay for some time.

The South Asian countries present some interesting contrasts. Sri Lanka in the late 1970s underwent a sharp albeit constitutional and peaceful change from a regime that was preoccupied with antipoverty efforts and social investments to one focused on economic efficiency and market adjustments. Each, however, intently pushed aspects of development until the country's smoldering ethnic problem began upstaging everything else. Bangladesh has undergone a series of violent changes of regime since 1972. Like Thailand but at a lower level of welfare and at a slower pace of improvement, Bangladesh has demonstrated considerable continuity in economic policy and responsiveness to the comparatively heavy role aid donors play in its beleaguered economy. No Bangladeshi regime could afford to be indifferent to the urgency of development.

Pakistan's economic record over the past quarter century has been strikingly regime-dominated. When Ayub seized power in 1959 he ended an era of sluggishness. He promoted exports, liberalized imports (although not as much as often believed), pushed agriculture and encouraged the private sector. In general, Ayub gave high salience to economic policy and endeared himself to the donor agencies. He fell ten years later, in part because of the social sector deficits and widened inequalities, including those between the country's East and West wings, over which his regime had presided.

When Bhutto took over at the time of the Bangladesh War and the partition of Pakistan, he developed a radically different relationship with the leading donors. At the outset he devalued the rupee and undertook to liberalize imports in a way that delighted the IMF. But then the new regime put on a (somewhat cosmetic) face of populism that involved nationalizations, some ill-considered heavy industry commitments and, most of all, a pattern of fiscal-monetary looseness that alienated the World Bank. The current regime's political case for aid picked up sharply with the Soviet invasion of Afghanistan at the end of 1979 and the subsequent influx of refugees into Pakistan. But economically Pakistan has evolved a more constructive relation with donors incrementally, introducing useful reforms in the realms of export promotion (if not yet import liberalization), agriculture, industrial privatization and energy. In the growth sweepstakes South Asian norms are lower than those in Northeast and Southeast Asia. Thus Pakistan's figures of 5.4 percent and 5.6 percent for real GDP growth during 1965–1973 and 1973–1983 respectively are the best for the region. The future may be troublesome however: the country has continued to accumulate real deficits in such areas as education, health, population policy and the enlistment of women in development efforts, and its institutional infrastructure is weak.

Finally, a word about the quality of government management of development in India. The conventional wisdom during the past couple of decades, espoused at least as much by Indian as by outside observers, has been highly critical of the government's role in Indian development. The government is said to have pursued the wrong (import-substitution) strategy and to have been excessively pro-public sector, regulatory and interventionist. There is no question, however, that throughout the past forty years, the government has been seized with development issues and has been manned by a number of highly trained and competent people. The conventional criticism of the record, although more right than not, probably is too doctrinaire, and Indian economic performance and prospects, bolstered by a set of development institutions stronger than those of its neighbor to the west, may now be on an upswing.

Resources and Policies

My thesis is that aid to Asia, although comparatively marginal and in most cases given for potentially distracting purposes, has had considerable success in promoting development. I have made some broad comments about the actors—the donor agencies and the recipient governments—involved in the aid transaction. There are a number of issues in the donor-recipient relationship that could be explored before the effects of concessional transfers in Asia during the past four decades are summed up. Indeed, all of the aspects of the donor-recipient relationship identified in Chapter II could be discussed in the Asian context. But there is not enough space for that, nor reason to think that all of the issues taken up in Chapter II are sufficiently different in Asia to require separate treatment. Accordingly, before turning to the results of Asian aid, I propose to consider only two key aspects—in fact, two dimensions so integrally related that they are a kind of dual aspect—of the aid relationship in Asia, the resource transfers that aid involves, and the influence on recipient policies that aid brings about. These twin dimensions of development assistance are very much in the limelight today, in this era of so-called policy-based lending. There is much interest, for one thing, in whether they can substitute for each other or instead are complements.

These two aspects of aid were present from the beginning in Asia but were not closely linked. The transfer of resources was a conspicuous aspect of all forms of development aid, with the possible exception of technical assistance. On the other hand, the technical assistance included in early Asian aid programs frequently had as one of its components the provision of economic and planning advisers, sometimes to such sectoral ministries as agriculture, but typically also to such centers of macroeconomic policy making as finance ministries and planning commissions. Thus there was, quite explicitly, an external input into macro policy. It often did not make that much difference whether the adviser was paid by the World Bank, AID or the Ford Foundation—his analyses and recommendations were likely to be compatible with the school of development doctrine espoused by the principal donors. But in the early years of the development promotion era, the donors' provision of grants or loans usually was not conditioned on recipients' adopting policy reforms favored by the donors.

One hypothesis about the linkages between resources and constructive policy change has been that the relationship is negative; the provision of external concessional resources has a crutch effect; it substitutes for internal saving; it postpones decisions by indigenous authorities to make painful needed policy adjustments; it delays self-reliance. Across-the-board allegations of this kind have been made in a few Asian country cases. They cannot be dismissed out of hand but are not very persuasive.

It is argued that the United States pumped resources into Korea in the postwar 1950s in a way that allowed Korea to pursue an ill-considered industrial strategy and temporize repeatedly in its adoption of adequate stabilization measures. Yet the United States felt it was strategically constrained to keep Korea economically viable, and its prostabilization efforts eventually bore policy fruit.

Aid—particularly the combination of World Bank and American bilateral ODA—is sometimes charged with providing Pakistan with a crutch that has weakened domestic resource mobilization in that country. The claim has some plausibility. At times ODA has funded a large fraction of Pakistani investment, and in 1983 domestic saving had dropped off to the derisively low level (considering the country's vigorous growth performance) of 7 percent. The latter compares with rates of 14 percent in Sri Lanka and 22 percent in India. However, in the early 1980s remittances from Pakistani workers in the Gulf states closed much more of the country's net-imports gap than did foreign assistance. Moreover, aid donors such as the World Bank certainly have not been cheerful weakeners of domestic saving; rather, they have pressed successive Pakistani regimes to improve that dimension of their economic performance for at least twenty years. The system's problem of resource mobilization seems to be deeply and internally embedded, not externally imposed.

The other part of former Pakistan, Bangladesh, has a somewhat similar problem. Its domestic saving rate is extremely low—a mere 2 percent—and its investment is overwhelmingly funded by external saving, mostly in the form of ODA. However, Bangladesh is genuinely and broadly impoverished. For 1983 the World Bank put its per capital income at only *one-third* that of Pakistan ($130 versus $390 in 1983 U.S. dollars). Bangladesh too needs to give increasing attention to resource mobilization, but it is hard to see how any promising growth sequences can gather momentum without further and more flexible development assistance.

Where the hypothesis of negative resource-policy linkages is far more straightforward and persuasive is at the sectoral level—specifically in the case of food aid. Clearly, there have been instances in Asia of food aid's having disincentive effects on indigenous food production. This was true, almost certainly, of the PL480 food that had been supplied to India by the mid–1960s. Without any of it, the political system might well not have survived the turmoil that urban food price inflation would have brought. But the increased supplies were overdone. The same evidently was the case at times in Bangladesh in the 1970s.

But this is one of the cases where aid managers have been learning, on both the donor and recipient sides. Whether they apply their knowledge successfully or not, they know how to avoid disincentive effects on internal production. The formula has been largely followed in India since the mid–1960s and can be used just as effectively elsewhere. It has two parts: first, when food aid is provided, a desired balance should be maintained between internal supplies and demand. If there are macro shortages, one may *want* to add more supply than demand. Otherwise, demand should be raised as much as supply, by giving the food to targeted groups, or employing the poor on labor-intensive activities or building stocks (all of these add to effective demand). Second, the donor must make sure that the recipient government in no sense slacks off on its promotion of internal food production; the food aid must not become a psychological crutch for the regime. (This was the rationale for President Johnson's "short tethering" of PL480 aid in 1965–1967. The procedure was ham-handed, but it strengthened those within the Indian government who were pursuing its new high priority for agriculture.)

The potential for positive linkages between aid's resource-transfer and policy effects increased as the 1950s proceeded. In a case like Korea, where the United States, almost by definition, was heavily involved in macro matters, the opportunity, indeed the need, for linkage did not have to be discovered; it was inescapable, and the U.S. authorities kept insisting on the need for stabilization and other reforms. But under Rhee the Korean authorities were slow to yield. In Taiwan the United States had the same involvement, and initially the government authorities were preoccupied with retaking the mainland. But they also were highly responsive to leads in behalf of liberalization, the private sector, land reform and agricultural development that, according to Jacoby, came in good part from the U.S. aid people.[17]

In South Asia there was a short period late in the 1950s when, as facilities for large-scale resource transfers (DLF and in 1960, IDA) were put in place, donors such as the World Bank and the United States seemed to be mainly preoccupied with transferring the quantities of resources needed to close arithmetic gaps in countries' development plans. But this quickly gave way to, or was amended by, a parallel emphasis on "self-help"—that is, on the importance of recipient policy changes needed to make both externally supplied and internally mobilized resources more effective.

At this point another lesson began to be learned. If policy "strings," especially macro policy strings, were to be tied (in those days the convention was to refer to conditions in this unceremonious fashion), it was hard to tie them to the project loans or grants that then comprised most aid. In the case of a project loan, the donor's capacity to exert influence on the recipient typically was exhausted in trying to affect the design and implementation of the project itself. There was seldom a residue of persuasiveness, as it were, that could be brought to bear on such general issues as subsidies, taxes and import regimes. A nonproject transfer of one kind or another was a much better vehicle for affecting sectorwide or economywide policies. Major donors put these findings to work selectively. USAID, for example, did a fair amount of nonproject policy-laden lending in both India and Pakistan during the mid–1960s. So did the World Bank in India (even though the Bank's general practice was tilted heavily toward projects). But the Bank did none in Pakistan next door, although it was advocating quite similar policy agendas in both countries.

There have been occasions in the Asian aid record when, in the course of supplying resources, a donor has provoked a recipient into adopting constructive policy changes as a matter of self defense. Such was the case in Korea in the early days of the Park regime. The United States, it will be remembered, had grown thoroughly frustrated with the Rhee government over the matter of stabilization. There was a brief honeymoon after Park took over in 1961; then in 1963–1964, after the government "went on a binge of spending and lending that precipitated a return of inflation,"[18] the United States imposed a set of harsh macroeconomic policy conditions on the continuation of its annual aid allotments. For the time being the Korean government had no option but to comply. But it bestirred itself to obtain substantial funding from Japan, the IMF and the World Bank in order to reduce its dependence on the United States. As seen by the combined Harvard-Korean Development Institute's study of the Korean development experience, this same determination to graduate from U.S. surveillance was a principal motive for Korea's adoption in 1965 of the outward-oriented policies that set the Korean economic miracle in motion and enabled the country to opt for reduced American aid.[19]

India was a different case. In the years 1964–1966 the Indian government went further in pursuing a pattern of aid-supported and conditioned agricultural and liberalization/devaluation reforms than most would have expected a few years earlier. I shall consider the results shortly. But for the moment the point is that when the liberalization and devaluation reforms were negotiated with the World Bank, acting in behalf of the Consortium of India-Aid Donors in the spring of 1966, the reforms were conditioned on the consortium's providing $900 million of new nonproject money. Although it was not written down, it was everyone's de facto understanding that this kind of funding would continue for the next several years. On the very first occasion for renewal, the Indians found President Lyndon Johnson of the United States reneging on what they thought had been a clearly understood deal. They not only were furious; they resolved never to let themselves be put over such a barrel again. Accordingly, they adopted extremely conservative fiscal policies over the next several years in order to build up a cushion of foreign exchange reserves against aid manipulation. This, in my view, was not a benign policy change; but it was a response to an unexpected cut in an external resource supply.

These two cases of conflicted donor-recipient relations were somewhat special. But there is also a more familiar way in which donors seeking to load policy influence onto their resource transfers let themselves be cast in an adversarial role. It has been well understood that donors almost never can force the recipient government into making a policy change that the recipient genuinely resists. If the change is made for cosmetic purposes it will not persist, and it will inject lingering rancor into the relationship. It is also well understood by all aid practitioners, however, that recipient governments, just like donors, are multifaceted, nonmonolithic entities. Thus the strategy of the external policy influencer must, almost invariably, seek to strengthen the hand of those leaders and officials of the government whose policy agenda the donor approves. And one of the best ways to do this is to play the role of whipping boy: those members of the governments with whom the donor agrees win arguments in intra-government debates by blaming politically distasteful reforms on the need to placate donor demands.

What might be called the "straight" cases of positive resources-policy linkage—those in which, as intended, resource transfers have been the vehicle for effective encouragement of constructive policy change—have, despite all the foregoing exceptions, been quite familiar in Asia in the past three or four decades. This, by all accounts, was the continuing character of the U.S.-Taiwan aid relationship for fifteen years. Although in Pakistan in the early 1960s the World Bank did not engage in much broad policy conditioning of its funding, AID did use nonproject lending to encourage a rather reluctant Pakistani bureaucracy (although not a reluctant finance minister) to follow up its new commitment to export promotion with a round of import liberalization in 1964. With a new round of troubles in 1965, however,including the brief Indo-Pak War of that year, most of the liberalization was soon aborted. In India at about the same time there was a concerted push by USAID and the Bank to use nonproject lending to help those in the government committed to a "new agricultural strategy" (leading to the so-called green revolution) and to trade and internal economic liberalization and devaluation to carry the day within Government of India councils.

As noted, American reneging on follow-on funding subsequently soured the Indians on the donors' role in the liberalization-devaluation exercise (although it was the subsequent Nixon-Kissinger tilt toward Pakistan in the Bangladesh War that was to fracture the bilateral Indo-U.S. aid relationship). Moreover, with the follow-on funding disappointment, the Indians, with exaggerated fiscal caution, backed away from, much of the liberalization. But the agricultural strategy emphatically stayed in place, as did the devaluation. Highly qualified Indian analysts found the latter, although flawed, to have been beneficial,[20] and the trend of Indian trade and industrial policy since 1966, although halting, has been quite consistently toward further liberalization. The policy-conditioning phase of the mid–1960s appears to have had lasting effects.

Other instances of resources-policy linkage can be found in the record of the World Bank/IDA relationship with India since the early 1970s. The linkage produced a kind of stalemate between the Bank and the Bhutto regime in Pakistan in the middle 1970s. The Bank refused to raise its low ceiling on Pakistani funding as long as the government refused to undertake of set of recommended macroeconomic reforms. Positive linkage between the Bank and Pakistan once again has been in forward gear in the 1980s as policy-based lending has been formalized in a structural adjustment loan and two or three follow-on sector loans.

A number of other instances of "straight" resources-policy linkages can be found in other periods and in other country parts of the Asian record. But for our purposes I must bring the subject to a close with two general observations.

First, the record reminds one that when the effectiveness of aid is being assessed, the instrument often is held up to unreasonable standards. For one thing, aid's impacts on policy can be episodic and still successful. Frequently there are useful ratchet effects in the ways reforms evolve, and (if we believe in self-reliance) it is not the business of an aid relationship to be everlasting. More particularly, in those cases where the donor country is genuinely committed to development promotion, whether its popularity with the recipient increases or diminishes is not a matter of great moment.

The second observation is this: more often than not in the Asian cases, resource transfers and policy influence have been complements, not substitutes. We have mentioned the possibility of aid becoming a crutch, and when ODA supplies become scarcer, there is always appeal in the thought of getting more bang for a buck—if only the recipient would adopt efficiency-augmenting policies, such reforms could be substituted for some of the aid that otherwise would be required. There can be such trade-offs, but where governments' commitments to development are reasonably serious and intelligent, they are rare. Sovereign governments continue to be proud. The donor, to get the recipient's attention, must buy a seat at the table. Or the reform he supports needs to be cushioned and facilitated by an increment of external resources. This was the position in India in 1967. Or, being already committed to a funding agenda adopted in earlier years, the donor, to encourage the adoption of innovative policies and programs, must have some spare financial capacity for new starts.

The Effects of Asian Aid Thus Far

Enough has been said to allow us now to draw the bottom line on the effects of ODA to Asia thus far with some dispatch. Aid certainly has not dominated the Asian development record. Across the set of Asian countries there has been no simple correlation of aid receipts and growth rates. Indeed, two of the so-called gang of four of Asian newly industrializing countries (NICs), Singapore and Hong Kong, have been virtually aid free, as has been, until very recently, another leading growth performer, the People's Republic of China. In general, compared in particular with that to Africa, the flow of aid to Asia has been fairly widespread and long lasting but thin. The volume of "Supporting Material to the Report of the Task force on Concessional Flows" provides an interesting comparison.[21] Whereas Asian countries were ten of the twenty-five largest recipients of aggregate aid over the period 1973–1983, only one (Papua New Guinea) was among the twenty-five countries that were the highest per capita aid recipients.[22]

Nevertheless, given the seriousness of both the donors and recipient regimes in Asia, aid has been useful and productive most of the time. As noted, there is comparatively little evidence of crutch effects, except in the case of some food aid earlier on. In 1966 Neil Jacoby hazarded the estimate that during 1950–1965 the U.S. aid program that was brought to an end at the close of that period had "doubled the annual rate of the growth of Taiwan's GNP, quadrupled the annual growth of per capita GNP and cut thirty years from the time needed to attain 1964 living standards.[23] One would hesitate to venture similar estimates for other Asian countries today. We would no longer be satisfied with the comparative simplicity of the capital-centered and foreign-exchange centered growth model Jacoby used. Moreover, Taiwan surely constitutes the best and clearest pro-aid country case. But there certainly have been cases (Korea during the

1950s, Bangladesh during the 1970s) where aid kept a country from collapsing into chaos. There have been cases (Thailand, Indonesia) where it has added a significant increment to a good average growth performance. There have been instances of delayed growth payoff, as with support to Korean education in the 1950s. Aid has had a hand in equity improvement (land reform and therefore income redistribution) in Korea and Taiwan as well as via employment programs and targeted consumption supplements in a number of countries.

ODA has had positive policy effects of the sort illustrated earlier. It has had major sectoral impacts—e.g., on the surface and ground irrigation and water management in Pakistan, on the green revolution in India, in the Pakistani Punjab and Southeast Asia including the Philippines. It has supplied more external funding for energy capacity than could have been had from other sources.

Of particular salience is the fact that aid donors have been effective in contributing to the building of key institutions in a number of Asian countries. In this context one can mention the Korean Institute for Science and Technology and the Korean Development Institute; management institutes in Thailand and the Philippines; from the CGIAR network, IRRI in Los Banos and ICRISAT in Hyderabad;[24] the Indian Institutes of Technology and the Indian (state-level) agricultural universities. A last note, not to be forgotten, is that the wide and numerous array of aid projects in Asia has fared at least as well on close evaluation as has the global generality of projects discussed in Chapter II.

To sum up: the facts that the ODA effort in Asia has been flawed, has had differing purposes and has been galvanized only intermittently should not be allowed to diminish its extreme usefulness.

IV. Looking Ahead

Development assistance policy in the United States in the past few years has maneuvered itself into a make-believe impasse. The impasse has become a political reality, is throttling aid to Asia, and it is likely to be unlocked only by executive leadership. U.S. bilateral aid, however, no longer is the pattern setter in Asia. There is an unprecedented opportunity now for Japan to take charge, mainly in the multilateral agencies. Meanwhile, most, but not all, Asian ODA recipients that have not already essentially graduated from ODA should do so in the medium term if supplies of concessional official finance can be augmented and trade access to OECD markets can be maintained or improved.

The Myth of Threadbareness

At this writing the U.S. bilateral development assistance program is subject to extreme financial constraint. In the Congress the leaders of the appropriations committees, jousting over the grand budgetary issues of defense, nondefense, taxes and deficits, are projecting sharp declines in the overall foreign operations budget. For its part the administration is pressing harder for military aid than economic aid, and on the economic side, harder for politically and strategically motivated "economic support" than for genuine development assistance. After protective earmarking of the appropriations for Israel and Egypt and our base rights in such countries as Spain, Greece, Turkey and the Philippines, and for Pakistan, what will be left for the rest of Asia and for U.S. contributions to the multilaterals on which Asia depends will be sharply down from inadequate recent levels.

Under present economic and political circumstances the American ability to produce ODA—especially, given the now accepted priority for Africa, ODA for Asia—is severely limited. Current polls indicate that the public is critical of and gives a low priority to foreign aid.[25] The public and their Congressional representatives doubt aid's effectiveness. And when domestic and other outlays with far larger and livelier constituencies must be sacrificed to deficit reduction, it is hard to find a budgetary forecaster who sees any lift in U.S. ODA for the foreseeable future. Few propositions in U.S. public affairs are more widely accepted than this just now, and few are less firmly grounded.

What is wrong with the idea that U.S. ODA is being inescapably squeezed by budgetary austerity is the same thing that is wrong with the proposition that a poor man cannot buy chewing gum. Unless he is absolutely impoverished—and the United States is not—chewing gum makes such a small claim on even a poor man's budget as to be trivial. Purchasing it remains a matter of discretion. Total U.S. ODA (for one comparison) is not much more than 3 percent of another category of the country's foreign policy spending, namely, its defense budget. ODA can be genuinely caught in a budgetary bind only when it is caught by a general budgetary rule being applied to many budgetary heads simultaneously. Such, of course, is the case today. Development assistance has a weak internal constituency in United States. When there is budgetary pressure, aid is one of the categories of spending most likely to be subjected to across-the-board cuts. But it is perfectly possible also, given the item's relatively small size, for it to be released from such lock-stepping and to be considered on its own merits. The choice is entirely a matter of executive and legislative priorities.

The Remaining Case for Asia

The case for continuing ODA to Bangladesh—and, on a smaller scale, to Nepal—is overwhelming. But unless there is a total collapse of U.S. contributions, these portions of the effort are presumably quasi-protected. The central issue is whether there can still be ODA for the better-performing Asian low-income countries—Sri Lanka, Pakistan, but most of all the two giants, India and China—in view of the urgency of Africa's needs. I will not undertake here to analyze the African claims. Rather, let us accept the virtually universal view: the priority for Africa is warranted. Stepped-up aid, especially in view of the fairly high per capita levels in Africa already, is by no means a sufficient answer to the desperate political-economic problems of much of the sub-Saharan region. But it is an essential part of the answer. Hence we can stipulate that it is ODA for the populous, well-performing, poor Asian countries that lies at the margin of development assistance planning for the next ten years. The purpose of the increase of ODA above present expectations that the Task Force on Concessional Flows recommended will be to keep development assistance for India, China, Sri lanka and (aside from strategic considerations) for Pakistan from disappearing very quickly.

As to the need that China, India and the others have for development assistance during the next several years, I cannot improve on the statement by the Task Force on Concessional Flows quoted at the end of Chapter II. It would not only be unjust to penalize good performance while the average level of poverty remains so great in the big countries, it would penalize aid's effectiveness. India and China now are among those countries best equipped to get good development mileage from net imports. Furthermore, to chop off ODA to these countries would catch them in the midst of a series of outward-oriented policy adjustments that particularly need foreign-exchange cushioning. And to force them toward the private financial markets in a big way just now might quickly collapse their good but only lightly used credit ratings.

In fact, the case for maintaining significant development assistance to the better performing Asian low-income countries (LICs) for the time being is so obvious that it is hard to believe that the United States is not charging ahead with it on geopolitical grounds. Our strategic interests in Indian stability are self-evident, not to speak of our concerns for the health of China's opening market economy. Equally it would be difficult to overlook what I have called our interest in "global systems maintenance" in jurisdictions numbering half the planet's population. With such stakes, even a myopic military planner should suspect that transferring $8–10 billion out of the U.S. defense budget to ODA, thereby doubling the country's contribution to the latter, would be strategically prudent. Along the same lines, it at least would be wise to trade some aid to Israel for aid to Asia, or to re-route much or most of our military assistance into economic assistance for the LICs.

Finally, one should not forget the magnified costs of a failure to move along one or another of these lines and escape the self-imposed noose that is about to throttle ODA for Asia more severely than ever. Most of that aid now flows through multilateral channels. Our multilateral colleagues are highly sensitized (we taught them the lesson some twenty-five years ago) to "burden sharing." As we cut back on our inputs of ODA to the World Bank and Asian Development Bank, they tend to do likewise, thereby magnifying the damage three- or fourfold.

Alternatives on the American Side

I have not quite closed the circle on my argument that budgetary constraints on ODA are largely illusory in the United States. They are so only if the President decides to battle for the needed program. In the second half of the second term of a president who has shown little disposition to give ODA a high priority, however, the administration seems unlikely to change its aid-claiming spots in any fundamental way. If one assumes that the ODA game will continue to be U.S.-centered as it has been in Asia and indeed worldwide, there are only a few alternative courses of action available.

For one thing, if the administration and some leaders in Congress are concerned about the near-term external-funding needs of the large low-income Asian countries but are not prepared to provide development assistance, they can at least increase these countries' access to nonconcessional official flows, such as IBRD and Asian

Development Bank "ordinary capital" loans. Such funding can quickly overtax the borrower's safe borrowing capacity. But it will be better in that regard than private bank loans—the terms will be somewhat softer and the availability more reliable. Thus there is a good Asian argument for expanding the callable capital of the multilateral development banks (MDBs) to accommodate increased nonconcessional lending. The Reagan administration has agreed to general capital increases to permit greater market borrowing and nonconcessional borrowing and lending by the MDBs "once it is needed." It argues that such a need is not imminent, but since the move would not have budgetary impact and would require only a change of timing, not of principle, in the administration's position, the White House may be susceptible to persuasion.

The second possible American (or American-centered) response to Asia's unrequited needs for ODA would have the same advantage of not requiring extra appropriations. Technically, meeting the ODA gap by a new issuance by the IMF of Special Drawing Rights (SDRs) could be a remarkably neat solution. With oil prices down and global inflation flat, the main substantive macroeconomic argument against the so-called SDR link in the past does not apply. A one-shot issuance of 5 or 10 billion SDRs would be a useful addition to global liquidity, but it would be a drop in the bucket; it would carry no credible inflationary threat. Moreover, billed and treated as a one-time exercise to meet a particularly difficult set of perceived constraints on ODA supply, the action would not intrude in any lasting way on the proposition that the function of SDRs is to provide liquidity, not promote development, and that their management should be left to the monetary authorities.

If there were a new SDR issuance in behalf of development, it would be done most feasibly in the near term via the so-called inorganic or indirect method. The distribution would be in accordance with IMF quotas, but then the OECD countries would agree to give part or all of their new allocations of SDR to IDA, which thereby, even with modest regular replenishments, would have comparatively abundant resources for meeting Asian and other LIC needs.

Regular SDRs these days, carry market-level interest rates. These would need to be lowered to afford the degree of concessionality that is appropriate for the poorer countries. This could be accomplished by asking the OECD countries which were transferring SDRs to IDA to give enough more to establish an interest subsidy fund that could be used to defray IDA recipients' interest charges.[26]

The sad thing about this attractive solution to the prospective Asian aid deficit is that it almost surely is not politically feasible. Probably in the United States it would take almost as much executive leadership to sell the SDR solution to Congress as it would a straightforward large increase in aid appropriations. The Reagan administration, like its predecessors, has been entrenched in its opposition to the SDR link; so have several other leading OECD govenments. There is no sign their positions have shifted.

For an American-centered scenario, then, that leaves only the choice of waiting for the next administration—of working on it pre- and postelection, first, to attach a higher priority to the purposes of development assistance, and second, to get it to understand the artificiality of the present budgetary barriers to doing what is needed on the ODA front, including in Asia.

The Japan Card

There is, however, another, non-U.S.-centered answer to the Asian aid gap that has begun to be widely if tentatively remarked during the past year. As noted, U.S. bilateral assistance has ceased being a pattern setter in most of the region. The question is whether the limitation on American ODA will continue to constrain the multilaterals. The opportunity is open, as, for example, ex-Chancellor Helmut Schmidt remarked to a Washington conference on the future of the World Bank in late June 1986, for Japan to take over the leadership of multilateral funding. I would add, particularly in Asia.

Schmidt made these points: Japan has an extraordinary propensity to save, which has expressed itself in a vast trade surplus and export of commercial capital. At the same time, it has by far the lowest relative defense burden in the OECD group. Yet neither its public nor its Asian neighbors would be likely to countenance a major step-up in Japanese military spending. One answer, said Schmidt, would be a radical increase in Japanese ODA.

Among prominent commentators within Japan, former Foreign Minister Saburo Okita has argued along similar lines. It would be unreasonable, he says, to ask the Japanese people suddenly to raise their propensity to consume. It would be more feasible for them to channel a larger fraction of their continued high savings into development assistance. Japan has in fact been raising its ODA. This has been evident in some of the detail on recipient countries noted earlier—for example Indonesia, Thailand and the Philippines. Indeed, as to its overall aid effort, Japan has committed itself to a succession of medium-term aid-raising targets beginning in the late 1970s (1978–1980, 1980–1985 and 1986–1992). In the latest of these efforts the government's undertaking is to achieve a level of disbursements in 1992 double (in dollars) that of 1985. Further, the government proposes to disburse more than $40 billion over the 1986–1992 period, and at the same time, to improve the quality of its ODA.

The point, however, is that all of the expansionism to date has been quite cautious. As a percent of the country's gross national product, Japanese aid averaged 0.22 during 1974–1976. With the first medium term target, the ratio rose to 0.32 percent in 1980. But then, as Japan's GNP continued to grow more briskly than those of the other OECD countries, its ODA/GNP percentage flattened. It receded to 0.28 in 1981 and 1982, edged up to 0.34 in 1984 and slipped back to 0.29 in 1985. Plainly, given the scale of its savings, which accounted for 31 percent of gross domestic product in 1984 (the highest for any OECD country except Norway) Japan is economically capable of a far more ambitious aid performance.

The needed improvement would have two dimensions. The volume of Japanese assistance would be raised sharply—enough to achieve some real movement in the ODA/GNP ratio. Secondly, most, if not all, of the increase would be in Japan's multilateral assistance. This would be essential if the reinforcement to volume were also to be as helpful as possible to ODA's geographic distribution. As noted, there is still a strong parochial (Northeast and Southeast Asia) tilt to Japan's bilateral aid. It would be more constructive for Asia overall, not to speak of the third world as a whole, for extra Japanese ODA to be fed through IDA's allocative machinery or that of ADB's soft loan operation.

There would be a further argument for going the multilateral route. Under pressures of the 1980s, bilateral aid programs have become more and more distracted and diluted by the commercial self interests donors have been building into their country choices, their project choices and the rest of their operations. The Japanese bilateral program, to say the least, has not been among the more self-denying in these regards. The way to avoid this sort of impairment of the development effectiveness on a Japan-supplied increment in ODA resources would be to put the latter through untied multilateral channels.

While making no forecasts, I would not be surprised to see some significant moves from the Japanese in these desired directions if two conditions could be met. First, the international community (and this, of course, includes the United States) would need to place ODA high on the agenda of subjects it has under continuing discussion with its Japanese partners. The most encouraging aspect of Japan's aid prospects is that serious proposals for expansion are arising from responsible and respected quarters within the country itself. But the government also is attentive to external opinions, especially when these are articulated officially from such sources as the other larger members of OECD. Hence it is important that aid expansion not be lost in the shuffle of all the other subjects—defense, trade, technology and investment—under discussion with the Japanese.

The other precondition if Japan is to step front and center in the multilateral aid arena, is an obvious one: As it does so, the country must be given a larger role in the management and governance of the multilateral financial institutions. One hopes that the Europeans and in particular, the United States are about ready for such a move at the World Bank. If they are, we will learn the extent to which, on behalf of the developing countries of Asia and elsewhere, the Japanese are prepared to accept the combined challenges of greater responsibility and greater leadership.

Beyond Aid

This piece has focused on the record of development assistance in Asia and has argued the need for increased assistance. However, it would be unfaithful to the intentions of both Asia's aid recipients and their donors to skirt the fact that both of them do still see concessional assistance as a transitory process. All Asian developing countries have three economic development objectives, not just two: growth, equity but also self-reliance.

This essay has discussed at some length two heavy recipients of aid, Taiwan and South Korea, that already have essentially graduated from ODA. Others will follow incrementally, first shifting to harder and harder blends of official nonconcessional with concessional transfers, beyond that to growing reliance on commercial finance. There are a few countries—Bangladesh is the most important case—where such an evolution has scarcely yet begun to unfold. But it is a natural sequence, and it is to be welcomed. At the same time, especially in the case of countries that have been making good progress, it would be foolish and costly to accelerate the process beyond the capacity of countries to keep pace.

Finally, it must be emphasized that the feasible speed of the transition out of and beyond ODA will depend heavily on the openness of the Asian countries to constructive direct foreign investments, on the effectiveness with which they promote their exports and on the degree of their access to OECD and other external markets.

For the time being, meanwhile, development aid still has a critical role to play.

Notes

1. To calculate the grant element contained in a loan-servicing scenario, the present value at the market rate of interest (conventionally assumed to be 10 percent) of each repayment is ascertained. The excess of the loan's face value over the sum of these present values, expressed as a percentage of the face value, is the loan's grant element.

2. Cf. John P. Lewis, "Development Assistance in the 1980s," ch.4 in *U.S. Foreign Policy and the Third World: Overseas Development Council Agenda 1982*, ed. Roger D. Hansen (New York: Praeger, 1982), pp.104–105.

3. OECD, *Twenty-five Years of Development Cooperation: A Review* (Paris, 1985), p.172.

4. Cf. John P. Lewis, *Quiet Crisis in India: Economic Development and American Policy* (Washington, D.C.: Brookings, 1962), pp.284–285.

5. The Task Force on Concessional Flows is part of the Development Committee that is jointly attached to the World Bank and the International Monetary Fund.

6. *North-South: A Program for Survival*, Report of the Independent Commission International Development Issues (Cambridge: MIT Press, 1980), pp. 244–245.

7. Appendix A, "New Means of Generating Future Concessional Flow," in *Aid for Development: The Key Issues*, Supporting Materials for the Report of the Task Force on Concessional Flows (Washington, D.C.: Development Committee, 1986).

8. OECD, *Twenty-five Years of Development Cooperation*, 1985.

9. *Report of the Task Force on Concessional Flows* (Washington, DC: Development Committee, 1985).

10. Robert Cassen, *Does Aid Work?* (Oxford: Oxford University Press, 1986).

11. Gordon Gray, *Report to the President on Foreign Economic Policies* (Washington, D.C.: U.S. Government, November, 1950).

12. U.S. International Development Advisory Board, *Partners in Progress, a report to the President* (Washington, D.C.: U.S. Government, March 1951).

13. In meetings of DAC, for example, it is interesting to observe a technical respect that is accorded representatives of USAID even as the other members are castigating the inadequacy of American aid appropriations.

14. For a comparison on recent Asian Development Bank and World Bank funding in Asia, see Gerald Meier, *Financing Asian Development: Performance and Prospects* (New York: The Asia Society, and Lanham, MD: University Press of America, 1986).

15. *Asian Development Bank Annual Report 1985;* also Asian Development Bank, *A Study of Operational Priorities and Plans for the 1980s* (Manila, 1983).

16. See Neil Jacoby, *U.S. Aid to Taiwan* (New York: Praeger, 1966).

17. Ibid., pp.137–138.

18. Edward S. Mason, M. J. Kim, D. H. Perkins, K. S. Kim, D. C. Cole, *The Economic and Social Modernization of Korea* (Cambridge: Harvard University Press, 1980), p.196.

19. Ibid.

20. Cf. Jagdish N. Bhagwati and T. N. Srinivasan, *India* (New York: Columbia University Press, 1978).

21. *Report to the Task Force on Concessional Flows,* Table I–8, p.22.

22. In this reckoning I count Jordan, Israel, Oman, Syria, Lebanon, the two Yemens, Egypt and Tunisia as Mid-Eastern rather than Asian or African countries. The group of twenty-five includes twelve Sub-Saharan countries.

23. Jacoby, *U.S. Aid to Taiwan,* p.152.

24. CGIAR: Consultative Group for International Agricultural Research. IRRI: International Rice Research Institute. ICRISAT: International Crop Research Institute for the Semi-arid Tropics.

25. A new 1986 poll together with the results of various other recent polls in other donor countries is contained in Christine E. Contee, *What Americans Think: Views on Development and U.S.-Third World Relations,* a public opinion project of Inter-Action and the Overseas Development Council. (Washington, D.C.: Overseas Development Council, 1987).

26. Cf. Richard Goode, *Economic Assistance in Developing Countries through the IMF* (Washington D.C.: The Brookings Institution, 1985).

Suggested Reading

Cassen, Robert, *Does Aid Work?* Oxford, 1986.

Dernberger, Robert F. and Richard S. Eckaus, *Financing Asian Development: China and India*, New York: The Asia Society, and Lanham, MD: University Press of America, forthcoming.

Development Assistance Committee, OECD, *Twenty-Five Years of Development Cooperation: A Review*, Paris, 1985.

———, *Development Cooperation 1986*, Paris.

Development Committee, *Report of the Task Force on Concessional Flows*, Washington D.C., 1985.

———, *Aid for Development: The Key Issues*, Supporting Materials for the Report of the Task Force on Concessional Flows, Washington D.C., 1986.

Jacoby, Neil, *U.S. Aid to Taiwan*, New York: Prager, 1986.

Lewis, John P. "Development Assistance in the 1980s," ch. 4 in Roger Hansen, ed., *U.S. Foreign Policy and the Third World: Overseas Development Council, Agenda 1982*, New York: Prager, 1982.

Mason, E. S., M. J. Kim, D. H. Perkins, K. S. Kim and D. C. Cole, *The Economic and Social Modernization of Korea*, Cambridge: Harvard, 1980.

Meier, Gerald, *Financing Asian Development: Performance and Prospects*, New York: The Asia Society, and Lanham, MD: University Press of America, 1986.

About the Author

John P. Lewis is professor of economics and public affairs at Princeton University, where he was also dean of the Woodrow Wilson School from 1969 to 1974. He has his Ph.D in political economy and government from Harvard and has taught at Union College and Indiana University. He was a member of the President's Council of Economic Advisers, 1963–1964, Minister-Director of the USAID Mission to India, 1964–1969, Chairman of the OECD's Development Assistance Committee, 1979–1981, and chair of the World Bank and IMF Development Committee's Task Force on Concessional Flows, 1982–1985. His writings have included *Reconstruction and Development in South Korea*, 1955; *Quiet Crisis in India*, 1962; (with Ishan Kapur) *The World Bank Group, Multilateral Aid, and the 1970s*, 1973; and several recent Overseas Development Council publications.